THE PAINTING ON
THE WINDOW BLIND

The Story of an Unknown Artist and a Daring Union Spy

Also by Neil Davis

NON-FICTION
Alaska Science Nuggets, 1982
Energy/Alaska, 1984
The Aurora Watcher's Handbook, 1992
The College Hill Chronicles, 1993
Permafrost, A guide to frozen ground in transition, 2001
Mired in the Health Care Morass, 2008

FICTION
Caught in the Sluice, 1994
Battling Against Success, 1997
The Great Alaska Zingwater Caper, 2004

THE PAINTING ON THE WINDOW BLIND

The Story of an Unknown Artist and a Daring Union Spy

NEIL DAVIS

iUniverse, Inc.
Bloomington

THE PAINTING ON THE WINDOW BLIND,
The Story of an Unknown Artist and a Daring Union Spy

iUniverse books may be ordered through booksellers or by contacting:

iUniverse
1663 Liberty Drive
Bloomington, IN 47403
www.iuniverse.com
1-800-Authors (1-800-288-4677)

ISBN: 978-1-4502-8240-6 (sc)
ISBN: 978-1-4502-8241-3 (ebk)

Printed in the United States of America

iUniverse rev. date: 12/23/2010

CONTENTS

⁓

Acknowledgments

Historian Dr. William B. Feis has contributed enormously to this document by providing me with commentary and archival material. Elaine Lundberg of Panora, Iowa, also helped much by locating documentation available in her local vicinity. I also am grateful to Rodney L. Hood for providing copies of drawings contained in his great-grandfather John H. G. Hood's sketchbook and biographical information on him. My wife Rosemarie contributed with discussions and reviewing of the writing as it went along. Carla Helfferich of McRoy & Blackburn Publishing also helped by editing a late version of the manuscript. I also thank Dr. Ronald Dewitt for a critical reading of the manuscript and help on locating biographical information on James Hensal. It has been a pleasure to work with appraiser Jane C. H. Jacob of Jacob Fine Art on this project, and I greatly appreciate her insights and the guidance she has given me throughout.

INTRODUCTION

This is the story of what started out as a simple search for information about a unique and previously unknown Civil War painting that I inherited some years ago. I had no idea when I started that the investigation would be become so involved and time-consuming, nor that it would be so much fun. The fun part was the pleasure and surprise of being able to uncover new information, bit by bit, about the creator of the painting and vastly more about its subject: James A. Hensal who served as Chief of Scouts under Union General Grenville Dodge in the latter part of the Civil War. In that capacity, Hensal led a part of what was considered to be the most important of the Union's counterintelligence operations. Not only that, he was a flamboyant individual, acknowledged by those who knew him as both reckless and fearless. "He was the bravest man I ever knew," stated General Dodge, long after the war.

I tell this story of the search somewhat chronologically in the way it happened, unfolding slowly over the course of five years, and mostly through use of the Internet and partly with the input of others. I took that approach because the search process I followed may be of interest to persons contemplating similar pursuits. These days, a great deal can be accomplished using the Internet, both for uncovering published and archival information, and also connecting with persons having previously unpublished information. Amazingly enough, new information about events of yore is popping up all the time, thanks to the ongoing digitization of long-forgotten books and documents that otherwise would continue to molder away in attics and on the shelves of libraries. But to get the complete story this is not enough, as I learned during the course of this investigation. A person also needs to have access to various county, state and other records. Being in Alaska, I could not conveniently pursue this avenue, but, fortunately, others did. I am particularly grateful to Elaine Lundberg of Panora, Iowa, who during 2010, very late in this investigation, uncovered in such records some of what I report here.

Also very late in the process, I happened to read the new book *The Grand Design* by Stephen Hawking and Leonard Mlodinow in which they discuss why the universe behaves the way it does. Part of their discussion notes that classical Newtonian mechanics properly describes the motions and interactions of objects we directly perceive in everyday life, but that when it comes to dealing with tiny unperceived objects such as atoms, electrons, and protons it is necessary to employ quantum mechanics.

A major difference between the two is that with Newtonian mechanics we can predict the locations and motions of objects exactly, whereas in quantum mechanics those predictions are based on probabilities and yield results that inherently contain a certain amount of uncertainty as to an object's location and velocity. To put it another way: In our everyday world describable with Newtonian mechanics we can be pretty sure we know exactly where objects are and how they will interact, but when we deal with tiny objects where quantum mechanics comes into play we can know their probable positions and behaviors to within a certain degree of precision, and we cannot know them exactly.

It occurs to me that there is a parallel situation when it comes to dealing with historical events. We can be quite confident when it comes to big events like wars or battles that we know exactly when and where they occurred, at least if they took place during recent centuries when multiple scribes were on hand to record the events. We know with certainty, for example, that the Civil War officially began on April 12, 1861 and ended on April 9, 1865, and the major battles are well documented. However, too often we lack exact knowledge of the details of the war's minor events and of the actions of individual soldiers involved. When searching for that information we drift off into the world of quantum history wherein we can only state with varying degrees of certainty what probably happened and who did what. Not many Civil War soldiers were shooting a gun with one hand and writing in their diaries with the other. What writing the participants accomplished usually was done well after the fact and therefore suffering from the vagaries of memory. Further complication comes when only second-hand accounts of oral information are available and those hearing and writing down those accounts have miscued in their interpretations of what was said. For these various reasons, we too often are left with incomplete or even conflicting accounts of events and individual actions. As will be seen in what follows, the consequence is that we are left with uncertainty and the necessity to state only what probably happened.

START OF THE SEARCH

⌒◊⌒

I t all started during an episode of the Antiques Roadshow one night in 2005, a century and a half after the events discussed here. My wife Rosemarie was watching the show that night in our home near Fairbanks, Alaska. Telling me about it later, she said, "They showed this painting of three cats by an unknown artist that was said to be a good example of American folk art. I did not think it was nearly as good as that old Civil War painting hanging in your office, but the Roadshow appraiser put a value of $30,000 to $40,000 on it. You really ought to try to find out more about that painting you have. It might be worth some money."

That was a new thought altogether because the painting she was referring to was one that we suspected was essentially worthless. About twenty years ago, the painting's owner at that time, my Aunt Louphena Hensal, was moving into an Iowa retirement home and needed to consolidate her possessions. She was going to throw the painting away unless I wanted to have it, and so Rosemarie and I put it in our car and took it to our winter home near Friday Harbor, Washington, and later brought it to our main residence in Alaska.

For a while we hung the painting on our living room wall because its seemingly odd nature made it a great conversation piece whenever we had guests. Most people were taken aback when first seeing the painting because, compared to the artwork most people display on their living room walls, this painting was a bit odd. It showed a man in a butternut long-coat holding a pistol as he looked backward over the posterior of the horse he was riding, an unreal one with short legs, a huge barrel chest and a foreshortened head. That this might be a stylized painting rather than one intended to depict its subject with photographic accuracy had not occurred to us or to almost everyone else who viewed it.

Seeing it for the first time, visitors usually commented on the picture. Their remarks were welcome springboards that usually launched me into telling what little I knew of the painting and its subject because it seemed to be an unusual and interesting story. The painting was said to depict an actual incident in the Civil War, and the guy on the horse in the picture was sort of a wild man who reportedly had killed his superior officer and gotten away with it. Not likely, it seemed to me and most listeners, but aside from that, we were also somewhat titillated by the fact that since the oil painting was done on a fragile old fashioned roll-down window blind it had survived more than a century in rather good shape.

The post-Civil War painting of James A. Hensal done on a window blind by "Bummer" Hood to depict an actual event: Hensal escaping from his camp as Confederate soldiers (out of sight) approach. In disguise as a Confederate soldier, Hensal is wearing a butternut coat. This is the only known painting of a Union soldier in a Confederate uniform.

WHAT WE INITIALLY KNEW ABOUT
THE PAINTING AND ITS SUBJECT

⌒⁄⌒

I had been told by my aunt and her husband Irwin Hensal that the painting did in fact depict an actual event. The man on the horse was Irwin's grandfather James A. Hensal, a northern spy who had served as General Grenville Dodge's chief of scouts during the last part of the Civil War. As such, Hensal played an important role in the war because General Dodge's scouts were recognized as a valuable part of his military organization.[1] In the painting, he is riding away from his campfire on the edge of a field looking back at Confederate scouts who have crept up during the night with the intent to capture him, but who are not actually shown in the painting.

The reason for the odd fact that the picture was an oil painting done on an old-fashioned roll-down window blind rather than on canvas or wood was part of the story that would unfold, and how that came about was part of the tale I would tell to whomever got me started off on this general topic. After mustering out of the Union Army, James Hensal had married and operated a farm he owned in central Iowa, some two miles north-northeast of the town of Panora. One day a man known as "Bummer" Hood who had served with Hensal in the war came along, destitute and needing a place to stay. Hensal felt very kindly toward Hood because he believed that Hood had once saved his life during the war, so he invited Hood to stay on the farm for a while. "Bummer" Hood liked to paint but lacked money for materials, so did paintings on the interior walls of the Hensal house (as was common in those days), and he had painted the picture of Hensal on a window blind signing it with the single word "Hood".

Many years later, after James Hensal had died and passed the farm on to his son Telford (Uncle Irwin's father), the old farm house was torn down in the late 1950s, and in the process it was discovered that underneath the wallpaper the house's ceilings and walls were covered with "Bummer" Hood's paintings. These were all destroyed and, as far as I knew, his only surviving painting was the one of Hensal he had painted on the window blind, and I did not know "Bummer's" actual name. (The house was near the small stream Bay's Branch that, several decades ago, was dammed up to create a 990-acre lake on what now is a bird preserve operated by the state of Iowa. A photograph of it published in the *Guthrie County Vedette* on July 18, 1957 and a map at the Guthrie County Historical Village in Panora, Iowa, show that the house was located on the low knoll beside the stream now occupied by the reserve's administrative buildings.)

I had become became aware of James Hensal and the painting of him much earlier, back in 1943, when I was eleven years old. My parents, on their way to Alaska to do wartime construction work, had sent my younger brother and me to live in Iowa with my father's sister Louphena and her husband Irwin. The Hensals had both been school teachers in Colorado until late in the Great Depression when Irwin's father Telford lost the farm he had inherited from James Hensal. Irwin and Louphena helped Telford Hensal buy another farm located three miles east of Panora, and then when Telford became too infirm to operate the farm, Irwin and Louphena stopped being Colorado teachers and became Iowa farmers. Irwin was a role model for me from the time I was three years old. He had a great sense of humor and was prone to playing tricks on people, especially on me. I thought he was having more fun in life than anyone else I knew. So I was happy to go to Iowa and live with him.

The James Hensal house on Bays Branch where "Bummer" Hood probably executed the painting of Hensal. James Hensal's grandson Irwin and Irwin's sister Dorothy are in the foreground, photographed about 1914.

By this time, the early 1940s, James Hensal was long dead, but I saw him every day because "Bummer" Hood's painting of him hung in the dark hallway just outside my second-story bedroom in the old farmhouse. Trips past him were frequent because the house did not have inside plumbing (and no electricity either). Usually I walked or ran past the painting without giving it any thought, but once in a while I would pause and wonder what it had been like back in the Civil War and the years afterward when James Hensal had farmed just a few miles from where his picture now hung. It had occurred to me that life on the farm near Panora for us was pretty much what it had been like back after the Civil War when James Hensal farmed.

Irwin Hensal and the author photographed by Louphena Hensal about 1936. She said that just before she took the picture I walked out in front of Irwin to see how he was posed so I could pose just like him—he was my hero.

Like his grandfather James, Uncle Irwin still farmed using horses or mules, but he did also have a small tractor, and he and Aunt Louphena, like almost all other farmers then, did have a car that they drove to Panora every Saturday night to go shopping and visit with neighbors. I recall only one family, a very poor one, who drove to town as James Hensal had done, in a horse and buggy.

Otherwise it was much the same: every farmer put one-third of his land in corn, one-third in oats, and one-third in alfalfa, rotating the crops each year on each tillable part of the farm in order to keep the soil fertile. They used no pesticides nor any fertilizers other than what came out of the farm's cows, pigs, and chickens. The produced crops mostly went back into the cows, pigs and chickens, and so any cash income came from selling the animals and their products, mainly eggs and cream extracted from milk with a hand-driven separator. Irwin, like his grandfather before him, was a member of an oat threshing run: a group of farmers who collectively owned a threshing machine and worked together, each day moving the machine from one farm of the run to the next during the oat harvesting season. (The threshing machine was powered by a steam engine that belonged to a member of the Hensal family, either James Hensal or a close relative. Once, during the transfer of the engine from one farm to the next it was left on the roadway overnight with its fire banked, and that night it blew up. A year or so later when a farmer living some two miles away was plowing his field he turned up the engine's whistle which had been projected to his field by the explosion. The whistle was passed down to me through my uncle Irwin Hensal, and I have it mounted on a boiler that I use on occasion to drive a small steam engine. The slightly damaged whistle makes an impressive noise when operated with steam at 100 psi. I also have an antique hog oiler that belonged to James Hensal.)

Life on the farm was mostly fun for an eleven-year old boy like me, although I had many daily chores to perform, and I had to walk each day to and from the one-room school located a mile north of the farm. (This was Cass # 7; the building now located in the Guthrie County Historical Village in Panora, Iowa.)

In the summer of 1944, my brother and I left the farm to join our parents who had homesteaded 14 miles down the Alcan Highway from Fairbanks, Alaska, at the site which is now the town of North Pole, but I returned to Iowa in 1948 to live again with the Hensals and attend high school in Panora. James Hensal was still there, sitting on his dapple horse in the picture hung just outside my bedroom door. When I left to go back to Alaska in 1950 after graduating from Panora High School, the picture was still on the wall. It stayed there until sometime in the late 1950s when Irwin and Louphena sold the farmhouse and moved to Fort Madison, Iowa, where Louphena again began teaching school and Irwin worked as a sociologist at Fort Madison Penitentiary. The picture went with them and remained there, basically in storage, until Louphena gave it to me and I took it to Friday Harbor about 1995.

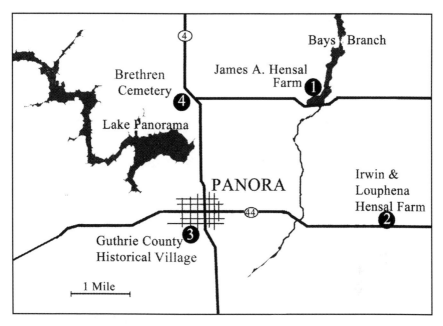

Sketch map of Panora, Iowa, area showing: 1—location of James Hensal farm where the painting was executed, 2—the Irwin and Louphena Hensal farm where the painting resided for many years, 3—the Guthrie County Historical Village where the painting now resides, and 4—the Brethren Cemetery where James Hensal and all other Hensal owners of the painting are buried, as is also John H. G. Hood's daughter Grace Hood.

THE APPRAISAL GETS UNDERWAY

⁓

Finally on June 10, 2005, our 54th wedding anniversary, I decided to follow Rosemarie's advice to get the picture appraised ("It's about time you start listening to me," she said.) I wrote a letter to an appraiser in Chicago that I had located on the Internet who offered to give a preliminary look at artwork for free in order to determine if an appraisal was called for, and if so it would be because the painting was worth at least three or four times the cost of the appraisal. Minimum appraisal cost would be $300. In the letter I included a picture of the painting, and when the answer came back the letter said the painting was worth appraising and that if I would send $600 the appraisal would be done. Hmm, $600; this sounded a bit like bait-and-switch, I thought, and worthy of checking out. So I telephoned the appraiser's office and got an answering machine—the appraiser seemed to have no e-mail address, either. Then I noticed a web page for an organization called the American Appraisal Association (AAA), and I checked the rolls of its approved appraisers only to discover that neither this appraiser's name nor his company was listed. I then picked out a name from the list of approved appraisers pretty much at random, but not quite, because the one

I chose was in Chicago, the general area of the country where the picture was from, and one of the appraiser's specialties seemed to be nineteenth and twentieth century American art. Furthermore, not only was this appraiser approved by the AAA, she was on its board of directors, and she had an e-mail address.

An exchange of e-mails then ensued during which I received a bit of education in the business of appraising antiques. It was a lot more complicated than I had realized, and I learned that an appraisal had to be performed for a specific purpose. Did I want to sell the painting? Did I want to contribute it to an art museum, and if so what museum, and would the museum agree to take it? The upshot was that this appraiser, Jane C. H. Jacob, and I signed a $850 contract for her to perform an appraisal for "planning purposes." If the painting had significant value and I later wanted to sell it or give it away as a tax-deductible gift then I would have to get an additional updated appraisal, and that would cost another $500. So be it; I by now had well over $1200 (the appraisal fee plus $400 I had spent in 2001 to have an art restorer in Seattle put a canvas backing on the fragile window blind) invested in a painting that might not be worth that much. Ms. Jacob was not willing to hint at any particular value for the painting, but she seemed to think its value was sufficient to merit evaluation. So I sent her a series of front and (pre-restoration) back photographs of the painting, and she would do the appraisal on the basis of those and whatever other information I could provide, and it would take about six weeks or so. (That turned out to be overly optimistic; the whole process would take nearly five years.)

At the outset, Jane Jacob stressed the importance of finding out more about the proper name of "Bummer" Hood, the details of his life, and also those about the subject of his painting, James Hensal, and the roles of both in the Civil War. That information could greatly enhance the value of the painting because major factors in determining a painting's value were the artist's reputation, the subject of his painting, date of execution, signature on the painting, and the historical significance of what the painting depicted. If the subject of the painting was a significant figure that fact could enhance the value by 25 percent, and if the subject was of historical significance it could enhance the value by another 50 percent.

So I then proceeded in the direction suggested by appraiser Jane Jacob—to find out more about painter "Bummer" Hood and his subject James Hensal. In a box of family papers I found several pages of handwritten notes my father Bon V. Davis had written in the late 1960s when he had visited Iowa and became interested in James Hensal. These notes and a few related documents are the basis for what I call here the family lore version of the history of James Hensal, his involvement with "Bummer" Hood, and his Civil War service.

Among the documents with my father's notes was a copy of the Cass Township portion of *History of Guthrie and Adair Counties, Iowa,* Springfield, Ill.: Continental Hist. Co, 1884. According to that document, James A. Hensal, was born in Adams county, Pennsylvania, September 10, 1837, the son of John and Anna (Cochun) Hensal. He came to Guthrie County, in 1856, settling on Section 22, in Cass Township, about two miles northeast of Panora. He went to Kansas two years later, in 1858, apparently keeping his farm near Panora but not returning there until after completing military service in 1864. In 1864 he went back briefly to Pennsylvania where he met his soon-to-be wife, Lovina S. Diehl, a native of that state whose parental home was on the Gettysburg battlefield. After they married they lived on the farm near Panora, Iowa. Regarding James and Lovina Hensal, the document states:

"They have four children living--Rollen, Elmer, Telford, and Minnie. They have also, three dead--Jennie, died in 1868, aged eighteen months; William, 1876, aged fifteen months, and Nora, died in 1881, aged sixteen years. He [*Hensal*] enlisted in the 7th Kansas cavalry, on the 10th of August, 1861, and was assigned to the Western Army, under Grant. He served in Missouri until the spring of 1862, when the regiment was ordered across the plains, but returned soon to the Mississippi, and participated in the engagements at Corinth, Iuka, Holly Springs, Grenada, and Jackson, Mississippi. Mr. Hensal was appointed a spy at Corinth, Mississippi, and served in that capacity with Sherman on the Atlanta campaign, and was promoted to the position of chief of scouts, in the fall of 1863. He owns two hundred and forty acres of improved land, and raises a large stock of cattle and hogs."

As the last sentence of that entry implies, James Hensal was a highly successful farmer after the war, and part of his success was due to the cleverness of his choice of a place to homestead: on Bays Branch, just northeast of Panora. The small stream provided ample water for livestock, and the soil there was a thick rich loam deposited by the last glaciation, about 13,000 years ago. Panora itself was exactly on the glaciation's southern boundary, a location causing the town to sit astride a demarcation in the nature of the landscape. This entire Iowa area had been glaciated some 100,000 years ago, but the passage of time had allowed extensive erosion of the glacial deposits to the south and southwest of Panora, leaving there a rough hill and valley topography. Then that last glaciation came along to cut and fill the hilltops and valleys north and east of Panora, leaving the gently rolling plain with rich soil on which Hensal homesteaded. He could not have picked a prettier place to spend his postwar years. According to lore, Panora derives its name from panorama, the pleasant hilly view a person gets coming in on the gently undulating plateau from the east and northeast.

My father's notes suggest that after the Civil War, James Hensal spent much time in Panora regaling the populance with his spying exploits during the war. He had the reputation of being quite a talker with a high ego and, most likely, a propensity for exaggeration. In this connection, a letter written in 1957 and surfacing in 2010 has relevant input. Its writer, Art Simpson of Des Moines said he knew James Hensal and as a boy had repeatedly listened to some of his tales in his grandfather Wagoner's store, one of the first business establishments in Panora. Simpson said that the stories "never got smaller" with each repeated telling. Simpson also noted that he was the descendent of a Confederate soldier, as were many of the early settlers of Panora: "the Jennings, Clines, Moores, Kellars, Carrothers, Nichols, and many more." Union soldiers had settled there too, and so there were many hot arguments in his grandfather's store, but no serious trouble, and all were good friends. That information was a lead-in to the story he told about listening, with other boyhood friends, to James Hensal's storytelling in Grandfather Wagoner's store when his mother Edith walked in. She said, "Jim Hensal, I want you to quit telling these boys such stories." Simpson said that James Hensal hid the bottle from which he was drinking behind a barrel and put his hand on her shoulder saying, "Now Edith, don't get mad. I am only trying to make good Yankees out of these boys." Art Simpson's mother replied, "Jim Hensal, you never was a captain, you never was a spy, you never was going to be executed, you never killed anything in your life but a lot of Reynold's rotgut. (Reynolds was the local druggist). Then as she left the room Art Simpson's mother said to Hensal, "Now don't forget you folks are supposed to come in a week from tomorrow for dinner."

However, James Hensal's local reputation spiked upward one day when he was standing outside a Panora establishment where he saw a newcomer riding into town. He recognized the man as one he knew during the Civil War from the odd way he sat his on his horse.

This man was now part of the Jesse James gang. The group had stopped in Panora to shoe horses (and was on its way to Northfield, Minnesota, where this man was killed during the bank robbery there a week or so later, on September 7, 1876). Invited into the store, the man verified at least some of the stories Hensal had been telling, and claimed him to be one of the bravest men he knew. He cited the fact that Hensal was known to ride Indian-style along ridge tops near Confederate forces to draw fire, thereby revealing their strength and location.

To me, the fact that Hensal had known or associated with a member of the Jesse James gang was interesting in itself, and I wondered which member it was and how the association came about. Looking into the matter I concluded that the man was probably Clell Miller or perhaps William Stiles, alias William Chadwell. Charlie Pitts alias Samuel Wells also was killed during the Northfield bank robbery, so he too was a possibility.

Family lore hinted that James Hensal was uneducated and had left home at the early age of twelve or so. According to his Union discharge document[2] compiled September 27, 1864, when he was 27 years old [*misstating his age as 23*] he was a small man, five-feet, seven-inches tall with blue eyes and brown hair. He was somewhat of a lady's man and also impetuous and fiery. According to one story, he had offered to employ his amateur medical skills in aid of a young neighbor lady who was abed with a sore abdomen. Hensal was indeed improving the lady's outlook on life when her family entered the room and, much disapproving of Hensal's methodology, threw him out. Another story was of an incident in Chicago where Hensal had gone long after the war to sell cattle. There he won $2500 in a poker game, but then accused the dealer of cheating and slugged him, whereupon the dealer's accomplices beat Hensal up and took away his winnings.

The most intriguing passage in my father's notes was a brief description of an event of unknown date and place in which James Hensal supposedly shot and killed his superior officer, was court-martialed and sentenced to death. As required before a Union soldier could be executed, Abraham Lincoln signed the death warrant. However, on the eve of the execution, fellow soldiers helped Hensal escape. He went off to join another regiment, and later served with distinction as a scout. As it turns out, this is not exactly what happened, but it would be nearly five years before I would learn that there was an element of truth to this strange story, but I defer going into that until later.

In addition to examining my father's notes I went on the Internet to try learn more about James Hensal and "Bummer" Hood since, being in Alaska, I was not in position to do much else. Searching on the name "James Hensal, I obtained one hit. Hensal was listed among those who had served in the Kansas Volunteer 7th Cavalry Regiment during the war. He was on the roster of Company B, and there also among the names of sixty or so others was a John H. G. Hood. Aha! Could it be, as seemed possible, that "Bummer" Hood was actually John H. G. Hood?

In an attempt to verify the association between these two names, I put in quite a few hours in front of the computer trying to learn more about Hensal and Hood, but not really getting anywhere. I saw ads for genealogy organizations that offered to trace almost anybody down—for a fee, of course. I did not bite on that, but I did find an organization called *FamilyTree* http://www.familytree.com that seemed to offer some free possibilities. It claimed to be an association of some thousand or so members who were searching for information on relatives. I found this organization because the name "Hood" was attached to one of its members. Back more than two years previously, someone identified as Rodney (Rod) Hood had put in an entry saying his family was from Iowa and he was looking for persons possibly related to John H. G. Hood. I could not contact him directly but could send a message to him through *FamilyTree*. I heard nothing for some days, and was not surprised because so much time had passed since his original entry. This was going to be another dead end I thought. Then a message came back through the system saying that Rod Hood was the great-grandson of John H. G. Hood, and it asked why I was interested.

I messaged back explaining that I had this painting, and I asked Hood if his relative had served in the Kansas 7th Volunteers and if he was of artistic bent. No answer; then I queried again some days later, and this time hit the jackpot. Yes, great-grandfather John Hood had served in the 7th, he was an artist and he had lived at Panora, Iowa, after the war—the location where the picture I had was painted. Almost certainly, we now knew who the artist was. Rod Hood's family at one time had another picture painted by John H. G. Hood, a very fine one, Rod said, of the Capitol Building in Des Moines. Unfortunately that painting had been damaged beyond repair and had been destroyed. Rod Hood thought that there might be other paintings of religious nature by John Hood in the possession of relatives.

Most significant, however, was that Rodney Hood had a 20-page pencil sketchbook that belonged to his great-grandfather. It was now faded and the pages were fragile and in poor shape, but Rod had them scanned and sent me files of the scans. Several of the pages seemed of little interest, but several others were rather nice. The stunner however was one drawing that obviously was the sketch on which the painting of James Hensal was based!

Page from the John Hood sketchbook containing the sketch that obviously was the basis for his painting of James A. Hensal. (Courtesy of Rodney L. Hood.)

By then I had also located Civil War historian Dr. William B. Feis of Buena Vista College at Storm Lake, Iowa, so I e-mailed him asking if in his researches he had ever run across the names of James A. Hensal and John H. G. Hood. Dr. Feis responded that he had not heard of Hood, but had seen Hensal's name in several places, most particularly in the writings of General Grenville Dodge housed at the State Historical Society of Iowa in Des Moines. He furnished me with copies of that information, and Rodney Hood also provided information on his great-grandfather John H. G. Hood. The following is an amalgamation of the information that by then I had located on these two gentlemen: Hood the painter, and Hensal the spy.

TWO CIVIL WAR SOLDIERS: HOOD THE PAINTER AND HENSAL THE SPY

John H. G. Hood	James A. Hensal
B. March 26, 1838,	B. September 10, 1837,
D. April 7, 1908	D. Dec 24, 1912

That James Hensal and John Hood did actually serve together in Company B of the Seventh Regiment Kansas Volunteers – Cavalry is shown by the following two extracts regarding them taken from the *Report of the Adjutant General of the State of Kansas, Vol. 1. - 1861-1865.* Leavenworth, Kansas: Bulletin Co-operative Printing Company, Chicago. 1867.[3]

John H. G. Hood of Berlin, Illinois, enlisted August 29, 1861; mustered as Private in Company B, September 15, 1861; promoted to Corporal October 5, 1861; promoted to Sergeant February 22, 1863; re-enlisted as First Sergeant January 1, 1864; mustered out with regiment September 29, 1865.

James A. Hensal of Leavenworth, Kansas, enlisted and mustered as Private in Company B on September 5, 1861; promoted to Corporal on November 24, 1961; mustered out on September 27, 1864.

Also listed here are entries relating to other members of the 7th Kansas Cavalry who figure in the story later on, but as a hint to what is coming, note that the first three are listed in the roster as "killed in action, January 3, 1963, at Somerville, Tennessee."

Fred Swoyer of Leavenworth, Kansas, mustered as First Lieutenant in Company B on September 15, 1861; promoted to Captain on October 5, 1861; killed in action, January 3, 1863, at Somerville, Tennessee.

Timothy Mullen, home unlisted and mustered in Company B on September 24, 1861; killed in action, January 3, 1863, at Somerville, Tennessee.

Edwin N. Butts of Wyanet, Illinois, enlisted August 12, 1861; mustered in Company H on September 3, 1861; killed in action, January 3, 1863, at Somerville, Tennessee.

Fletcher Pomeroy of Wyanet, Illinois, enlisted August 18, 1861; mustered in Company D as Private on September 3, 1861; promoted to regimental Q. M. Sergeant on August 1, 1863.

George W. Kenan of Lexington, Missouri, enlisted on January 1, 1864; mustered a Private in Company A on January 22, 1864; mustered out with regiment September 29, 1865.

The Company B roster shows that Hood and Hensal enlisted within a week of each other (August 29, 1861 and September 5, 1861). Hensal is listed as a member until mustering out on

September 27, 1864, but Hood re-enlisted and served until the regiment mustered out on September 29, 1865. According to this roster, Hood rose rapidly up to the rank of sergeant, whereas Hensal never achieved a rank higher than corporal. That seems odd in view of the fact that Hensal later (in late 1863) became Chief of Scouts under General Grenville Dodge while still being listed as a corporal in Company B.

In one place, the roster erroneously lists Hood's residence as Berlin, Illinois, and in another as Berlin, Iowa, instead of the proper New Berlin, Illinois. These minor errors serve as a warning that what we may deem as being official records are not always correct or descriptive of actual events, and we will see that other discrepancies of similar nature surface in what follows.

John H. G. Hood's Whereabouts Postwar

⁓

It was desirable to pin down the actual date Hood did the painting of Hensal, since my dad's notes said only "about 1870." So I was very interested in what Hood's great-grandson Rodney L. Hood could tell me because his whereabouts after the war were relevant to this issue. Rod sent me information that I summarize below.

John Henry Gray Hood (also known as Henry G. Hood and H. G. Hood) was born between October 1837 and 1838, at Lynn, Massachusetts, where several generations of his family had lived after emigrating from England. At approximately age 22, in about 1850, he migrated westward to New Berlin, Illinois, his listed residence when, in September 1861 at Lawrence, Kansas, he joined the Kansas 7th Calvary Regiment. He was mustered out at Kearny, Kansas, on September 29, 1865. According to the 1870 Iowa Census, he was living at Tabor, Iowa, with wife Harriet A. M. Lewis and first-born child Edgar, age 10 months. Hood and his family moved to Carroll, Iowa, in about 1875 where their second child Grace was born. The family traveled from there north to Buena Vista, Iowa, where several more children were born, then back southeasterly approximately 100 miles or so to Carroll, Iowa, and then, in 1892, approximately 50 miles east to the neighboring town of Panora, Iowa.

An obituary of his daughter Jessie Mae (Hood) Montgomery stated that she was born at Neola, Iowa, May 18, 1877, and implied that John Hood and his family moved to Panora in 1894, not 1892 (*Guthrie County Vedette*, Panora, Iowa, April 29, 1953)

Census records as supplied by Rod Hood are as follows:
JOHN HENRY GRAY HOOD , alias HENRY G. HOOD:
Census 1: June 22, 1870, Tabor, Fremont Co, Iowa
Census 2: June 1880, Storm Lake, Buena Vista Co, Iowa
Census 3: 1895, Panora, Guthrie Co, Iowa
Census 4: 1900, Panora, Guthrie Co, Iowa.

Rod Hood said that his great-grandfather was a painter/ artist by profession, and most of the census records list him as such. Various obituaries and other documents claim he was of significant talent, making his living selling his paintings and doing commercial art work advertisements for businesses. Several of his eleven children, including his eldest daughter Grace, also were artists. Grace died at Panora in 1950. Her obituary published in the *Guthrie County Vedette* that year states the following:

Grace was the oldest daughter of a family of eleven. John Henry Hood, her father, and his wife Harriet, moved into Panora in 1892 [*Harriet died in 1891, so was not part of the family move to Panora*] and, together with her family, Grace became a moving spirit in the early history and erection of the present Presbyterian church.... Miss Hood was considerable of an artist, leaving behind many beautiful paintings.....She assisted her artist father in decorating the opera house that stood a number of years in Panora. Many of the old-timers still remember its dignity and beauty at the hands of the artists,

At the redecoration of the church which she loved and was a member, it was the wish of Grace that she might herself renew the work of her late father, to bring back the artistic beauty of the past, but God willed she should join the eternal society of artists, to paint into nature the undreamed of beauty of the firmament.

******

John Hood's obituary appearing in the *Gazette Reporter*, Neola, Iowa, on April 16, 1908, refers to him as "Capt. H. G. Hood, formerly of Neola, Iowa, but recently of Panora, Iowa," and states that he died at his home there Thursday April 7, 1908."

Regarding this issue of the date of the painting, oral information passed down to me through the James Hensal family (son Telford Hensal to grandson Irwin D. Hensal to Louphena (Davis) Hensal to me) strongly suggests but does not explicitly state that John H. G. "Bummer" Hood temporarily resided at the Hensal farm outside Panora, Iowa, shortly after the end of the Civil War, that is, sometime after 1865. However, the Iowa Census (see above) states that by 1870 Hood was living at Tabor, Iowa, in the southwestern part of the state. My father's notes on Hensal oral history state that Hood's painting of Hensal was done "about 1870." So it appears most likely that the painting was done sometime in the interval 1865-70. Of course it is possible that Hood did the painting of Hensal after 1892 (or 1894) when he moved back to Panora with his passel of ten then motherless children. The family notes on Hensal history make no mention of Hood having a family when he first came to the Hensal property. The Hood sketchbook is of little help on this issue because it appears to contain mostly undated sketches probably made as early as 1864 as well as those made much later: after Hood took up residence in Panora and was doing commercial artwork there.

Following are reproductions of several pages of John Hood's sketchbook:

The cover of John Hood's sketchbook. Courtesy of Rodney L. Hood.

Page of Hood sketchbook containing the sketch portrait of General William Tecumseh Sherman, presumably made in May 1864, although the date "July 22nd" appears in the upper-right corner, and that is the correct date of the battle of Atlanta. Courtesy of Rodney L. Hood.

A page of the Hood sketchbook showing what appears to be a commercial sketch. Courtesy of Rodney L. Hood.

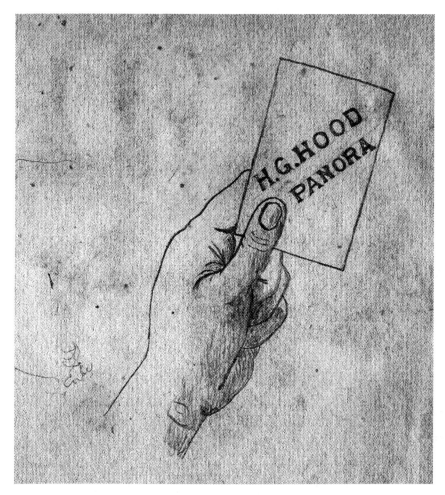

A page of the Hood sketchbook presumably drawn during the period when John Hood was living in Panora. Courtesy of Rodney L. Hood.

HOOD'S AND HENSAL'S
EARLY WARTIME SERVICE

⁓

B ecause I knew so little about the Civil War at the start of
this search, I was slow to see the implications of the fact
that John H. G. Hood's nickname was "Bummer" and that he
and James Hensal had joined the ranks of the Kansas 7th Cavalry
Volunteers near late-August 1861. As it turned out, pursuit of
the term "bummer" and the origins of the 7th Cavalry led to
some interesting information about both Hood's and Hensal's
probable activities early in the North-South conflict. I found
that "bummer" has several meanings, the most common now
being something bad, as in: "It was a bummer that I had to get
caught sleeping on the job." Another meaning during Civil War
times was that it was the name of a long-coat often worn by
officers of that era. Most likely, however, is that Hood received
this nickname because he was among the men who did foraging
work to supply the army, and they were called bummers. They
gained fame for the pillaging they did in Kansas and Missouri
prior to and during the early part of the war. The most notorious
"bummers" of the Civil War were the persons who became
members of the Kansas 7th Cavalry Volunteers, and especially
those in Companies A and B, who it seems were the worst of all.

Both Hood and Hensal were among the approximately forty or more members of Company B.

Perhaps for good reason, it seems that neither Hensal nor Hood have left any commentary regarding their activities during the months surrounding the time when they officially became members of Company B of the Kansas 7th Cavalry near the end of August 1861. Nor is it known if either was involved in the conflict prior to that time. They might well have been, and in that connection it is odd that Hensal left his Iowa farm in 1858 to go to Kansas. That he was there in 1860 is verified by the census of that year. It states that he was a 21-year-old carpenter living in Easton Township, Leavenworth, Kansas Territory. It seems strange that a young man would homestead in central Iowa, then shortly thereafter leave for central Kansas. Was he so adventurous that he went there intending to become involved in the erupting hostilities?

This might well have been the case, because the Civil War was underway in unorganized fashion in Kansas and Missouri in 1858 well before its official start date of April 12, 1861, when Confederate President Jefferson Davis ordered the attack on Ft. Sumter in South Carolina. Kansas was settled in the 1850s by both pro-slavery advocates and abolitionists who were at odds over the issue of whether Kansas would be admitted to the Union as a free or pro-slavery state, and that led to violence between various guerilla bands claiming allegiance to one side or the other. Those on the pro-slavery side in Kansas and Missouri became known as Bushwhackers and their opponents were called Jayhawkers. The term Jayhawker comes from Jayhawk, a mythical bird combining the qualities of the noisy, quarrelsome, nest-robbing jay with the stealthy, hard-striking sparrow hawk.[4]

One of the better known Bushwhacker groups was that of William Quantrill, called Quantrill's Raiders, comprised of semi-legitimate soldiers acknowledged as such by the Confederacy. Relevance to the story here comes about because tagging along with this group were Frank and Jesse James and their cousins, Coleman and Jim Younger, who later formed the notorious James Gang, and at least one member of that gang was known to James Hensal through his association with him at some time before or during the overall Civil War conflict.

However, as members of the 7th Kansas Voluntary Cavalry Regiment, both James Hensal and John H. G. Hood were Jayhawkers. The group they belonged to was originally organized in early August 1861 by Colonel Charles R. "Doc" Jennison, and was commonly referred to as Jennison's Redlegs. The part of that group Hensal and Hood joined soon came under the command of U. S. Senator James Henry Lane. Consisting of about a thousand men, this group known as Lane's Brigade, officially became the Seventh Kansas Cavalry Regiment of the Union army under the field command of Daniel R. Anthony on October 28, 1861, roughly one month after both Hensal and Hood had joined it.[5]

The Kansas 7th Cavalry quickly gained a reputation for its plundering escapades in Missouri and Kansas. "It was little more than a mob of thieves and adventurers who in the late summer and fall of 1861 went on a looting and burning rampage in western Missouri," stated one historian.[6]

Hensal and Hood evidently had intimate involvement in all that, and in the first serious battle in the western region, one fought on November 11, 1861 on the Little Blue River near Kansas City. Commanding officer Daniel R. Anthony ordered Companies A, B, and H (the three mounted companies of the regiment at the time) to attack a rebel encampment under the command of Confederate Colonel Upton Hayes. They drove the rebel group from the camp, and it made a stand on nearby hills. "After a furious struggle, in which nine of his little force were killed and 32 wounded, Colonel Anthony, after burning the rebel camp and capturing all their horses, withdrew from the field. The regiment subsequently took part in several other engagements in the same locality," stated one writer.[7]

The Union high command was not pleased with what was going on out there in Kansas and Missouri. According to one writer, "By 1862, Kansas First, Third, Fifth and Seventh regiments were cited for plundering. The Seventh Kansas was so bad that its commanders Col. Charles Jennison and Lt. Colonel Daniel R. Anthony were removed from command and the regiment sent to Corinth, Mississippi in the summer of 1862."

HOOD'S AND HENSAL'S
LATER WARTIME SERVICE

⤳

H ere the trail ends on what I have learned about any specific
Civil War exploits of artist John H. G. "Bummer" Hood,
but there is much more on the subject of his painting on the
window blind, scout James Hensal.

Both men apparently were with the 7th Kansas Cavalry when it
moved from Leavenworth to Humboldt, Kansas, in January 1862.
It remained there until late March and then went to Fort Riley,
Kansas, in late April, where it prepared to travel overland to New
Mexico. The plan changed, and the regiment went to Lawrence,
Kansas, and then back to Leavenworth where it was ordered to
travel onboard transports to Pittsburg Landing, Tennessee. Again
the plan changed, and the regiment disembarked at Columbus,
Kentucky. There the regiment remained until June 7, 1862,
performing escort duties for work parties engaged in repairing
the Mobile and Ohio railroad. The regiment arrived at Corinth,
Mississippi, on July 10 and operated in the general area shown
on the accompanying map for some months thereafter. One of
the more notable engagements Hood's and Hensal's Company
B participated in was the battle of Iuka fought on September 18,
1862. General Rosecrans specifically cited the company and also

Company E for bravery during that battle.[8] Information about James Hensal's activities at about this time surface in a letter he wrote to General Grenville Dodge in 1907.

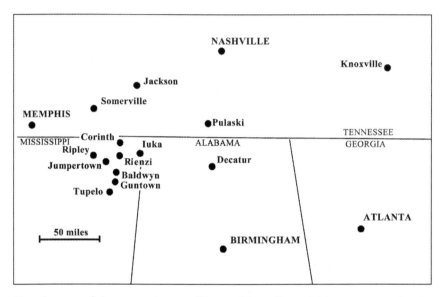

Sketch map of the general area of James Hensal's activities commencing in summer 1862. It shows the locations of many of the towns mentioned in the text.

JAMES HENSAL'S LETTERS TO GEN. GRENVILLE M. DODGE, 1907 AND 1869

⁓✼⁓

Geneneral Grenville M. Dodge's papers archived in Des Moines, Iowa, contain two letters that James Hensal had written him long after the war. One written in 1907 describes an event occurring more than forty years earlier. In it, Hensal displays considerable phonetic ingenuity in his spelling out the details of that event. The version given here is an OCR scan. The original is typewritten double-spaced, eleven pages long. I have tried to correct for OCR artifacts without altering the wording of the letter, but I have altered the spacing of words and retained the original pagination. The copy I scanned suggests that the letter was signed James D. Hensal, whereas all other references to Hensal list him as James A. Hensal or simply James Hensal. This probably is just a machine or transcription error. The letter:[9]

General Sir:

Since mother past away my hired man & I are alone tryinge to feed this stock out & get it ready for market. I have 6 car loads cattle & hogs. I intende to ship some time in April to Chicago, then I will cleane up & quit farming, purhaps travel some.

39

General, I am goinge to give you a ride that you know nothing about at least I dont think you do. Oald saying is it was a ride for life. just before the battle of Juka [*Iuka*] was fought [*September 19, 1862*], my Capton drew his sholder straps to give me a liken. The Capton was six feet & 3 inches tall but he never puled his sholder straps agen for the Boy. [*This was Captain Fred Swoyer who the record states was killed in action January 3, 1863 at Somerville, Tenn.*] I was an nun comisson officer at the time. he then put me under a rest but go whare I pleased. We fought the battle of Juka [*Iuka, fought September 19, 1862*] & then Corinth [*fought October 3-4, 1862*]. after that Company A & B was ordered to riensa [*Rienzi*], for scouting under Col. Mursie [Lt. *Col. Augustus Mersy, a German-American in command of the 9th Illinois Infantry.[10]*], com B was my Com, it was when Gen. Grant was geting ready to open Miss railroad to go to Vixburg, thair come a dispatch to Murser [*Mersy*]to sende those too companies amediately to Corinth & join thair regement & take the advance on to Holly springs.[*Holly Springs*] When the order come Co A was out on a scout. A dispatch had to go to call them in, the Capton called 4 diferent men to take the dispatch & go. they refused goinge. he then called the boy jmmie as he always called me. now this was the first duty he required of me sinse he laid

-page 2-

his sholder straps for me. Then he called me he wanted to know wheather I would go. I toled him yes, Capton, I will go. When he toled me whare I had to go I new it was a rockey road to travle. it had to go to jumper town

[*Jumpertown*], or some whare in that vacinety or in short I had to hunt them up. When I toled Sonyer [*Swoyer*] that I would go he said he would sende those 4 felows alonge with me for punishment. I then refused to go but toled him I would take the dispatch & go a lone. Dodge, sir, I knew if I got through it would bee a merical. I had to run what was called the gentlet. I had to ride within too miles of baldon [*Baldwyn*] & guntown whare too thousand rebles lay. Rippley [*Ripley*] was to my right. The rebles scouted it day & night watching our men at Corinth to notifye Price & Vandorne [*Van Dorn*] lying at hollysprings. While jumper town lay 15 miles about west of riensa [*Rienzi*]. Now for the ride. I mounted my horse, reported at head quarters. It was 9 oclock at night just a tatoo beat for lights out. Merser [*Mersy*] threw the war map down & shoed me the rout. I never had beene to jumper town. I looked it over & then Murser bid me good by, he called the officer of the night & sent him with me to the out post to let me out. In goinge to out poast the capton said young man whare are you goinge. I toled him to jumper town. young man you will never see camp agin. I remarked that one man dident know it all. well, that is so, I glory in your spunk. thair is one thing I will ask of you to do for me & that is to whirl on your saddle & take the last look of camp. I re-

-page 3-

marked all right Capton. I did. it was a moon light night; as the Capton spoke to the sentnal, let this man out he remarked fair well young man for the last time. I raised my beavor & slashed the spurs & away I went. I will stop off a little here. I new that capton new somthing but afraid to tell me for feare I wouldent go but he dident know his man. thare was a curior come in about sun down& 30 rebles after him. I was toled afterwards if the curior had a nother quarter of a mile to make the jonnie would of got him. the pickets fired on the rebles & saved him.

Away I went. I come to a house & hollared, the oald man come out. Am I on the right road to jumper town. Yes son when you get down to corner of my field bare to your right, dont go strait a head, that will take you to balden & guntown. I new that much enny way. When I got to the corner of the field I was then in open timber. This road through the timber was a corderoy road, it was about quarter of a mile long. just as I got over road thair was a bridge to cros, high in the senter this bridge was about 12 feet wide & just half of the bridge toren up from the same side I was coming. after you crossed this bridge you struck a hill & a worm fence to your left on top of hill a cotton ginn. When I road up to the bridge & sene it toren up my first thought was to dismount & pull the planks up. thay ware all

-page 4-

shoved off to the right & stuck up about a foot above the sleeper. I changed my mine. if I did I am gon up. I turned in my saddle sene an opning in the timber, thinks I can cross this revan. hire up I whirled my horse & road about 6 paces back then turned into the timber on my left. I maid a half sircet. thair was a big tree to my left, just as I glansed at it I imgion I seene a man lyiuge flat on the ground behined this tree. I took the second look then I sene it was a man. just then I looked towards the bridge. thair I seene a nother one lyinge. thinks I the arkangles & the devills are all out to night. I road up to the revean but it was a leep in the dark. I couldent tell the deph or the width all covered with bramble bushes. I droped the rain & give him the spur. he threw his head side ways & snorted & run back. then I new they ware lyinge under my horses neck. thay ware laying in ambush for this scouting party. When my horse run back I pulled my revolver, the rabs jumped too thair feet & cocked thair double barrel shot guns. halt you son of a bitch rung out at midnight our, or I will shoot you. hold on thair cried the boy on horse back or the target as you may call it. hoo in hell are you eneway ridinge around through the timber after night. the rider responded that is none of your d. d. business. this is supose to bee a free country. you now dismount or I will blow hell out of you. hold on the target hollered, dont bee in such a

-page 5-

hury about shooting. Why you would shoot one of your one men. You are excited. I new soldiers to shoot thair one men thruh excitement just like'you. Well hoo in hell are you enyway. do you want to know the target aske. Yes I belong to the 7 Kansas, dam you. then the fun comensed. thay both threw up thair guns & took aim at the target. they had just 4 shots. I sited thair pieces, they ware leveled for my head, thay ware the bigest shot gunns I ever sene. i am goinge to shoot, dismount. go to hell & I threw my self on my left sturip cleane from off the sadle. he tore away & I at him with my revolver. I stratened quick & threw my self on my right sturip. I then slackened the rain & dug the spur in him. he rared up & leaped into the road, just

43

as I threw myself second time on the rite side of my horse the other man fired at me. when the horse leaped into the road & turned homeward I threw my self on my left sturip cleane to his left side. just as I threw myself last time they fired the other to shots after me. I then stratened up, my horse farly flew & so did I. I think I was a little a head of my horse the hole way back to camp.

Now, General, this shootine all took pace in side 40 feet. What saved my life was my activity me purforming jim nastick feats upon my horse. I could ride equal to a Comansie [*Comanche*]. A nother thing is I was so close too them thay always over loaded

-page 6-

them shot guns in close qorters.

Well, General, back to camp I went. woak up Murcie [*Mersy*] & toled him what hapened. When I went in to his tent it all most nocked me down the smell of whiskey. then the old german began to pray in dutch till the tent began to flap & the oder from that whiskey stomach enough to kill anny man. to hell mit the reps the old gurma utered. Well jayhalker I know a nother road, will you try it agin. I will, I answered, but General I must have another horse, mine is run down. god bless you jayhalker, you shal have the best & fastes horse in camp. give me youre hand. now you go to your company & tell your Capton to give you the fastes & best horse on the line & tell him to come up here. I did as I was ordered.

When I woaken up the Capton, then thair was a nother prayer but his was in inglish. I had mu sabour on. I toled the capton I dident want it but I wanted a nother revolver.

44

All right I will give you one of mine. I took the sabour off, then I had too revolvers all fresh loaded. the capton toled me to take sargent Jesup horse, he was a fine looking horse & speady. [*No doubt refers to First Sergeant Andrew Jessup who, according to the official record, deserted at Germantown, Tenn. February 8, 1863*] I informed the capton that he would have to tell the sargent about it. he did, then the hevens opened. the sargent was a big man ab out 200 pounds. the sargent swore I couldent have the horse. the too

-page 7-

was about to fight over it. I stept up & soone settled it. I caled the sargent by name & remarked, you would rather ride that horse your self. Yes, he remarked, you are just like me, here is the dispatch. take it & go. I went one trip. I am not ancious to go a nother.

you godam little fool, you take the godam horse & kill him. he run back to his tent & I after him. take your one horse & go, you dam coward, go & take the horse. I bee darned if I want to die out thair in the woods like a dam dog. So that ended the figh betwene him & the capton. the capton started for head quarters & I sadled & bridled the horse & swung my self into the saddle & started for head quarters.

Col. Murcie [*Mersy*] threw the war map down & pointe out the road, him & the Capton bid me good by & god spead. I mounted & away I loaped. the moon was shing bright, it was about full. the roads was dry & dusty, the horse was fresh shod & clatter of his feet rung out through the stilnes of the night & ecoed through the timber onse

& a while an owl would brake the stillnes of the night, but it wasent long till the stillnes was broake in reality. I kep my eye on my horses ears. I new he would here anny thing before I would or as quick. I was nearing cross roads whare Col. Murcie toled me to look out, for hell, he remarked, the rebs keep it scouted day & night. I noticed my horse throwing his nostrells in the air

-page 8-

& snort. As I quickly rained him to keep still I hurd the nois, about the same time I was nearer those cross roads suner than I though I was. then I began to prepair for battle. I new if I was taken a live it was death. When A 7 Kansas man was taken it was shure death. I will say right here I wore that night a gray overcoat that help me out some that night. I drew my revolvers. I poot one of them under my left thie so if I empied the one I could grabe other one in a hurry. up I road to the cross roads. those cross roads was in timber. I road up as brave as a lyon. thay hollared hoos thair. then I shouted the yanks, the yanks, bang, bang, I let drive in the air over thair heads. I soone cleared the way. And on I went. the timber rung with horses in every direction. I slaped spurs & urged my horse faster. Well, I maid the first run by puting on brass or in other words I had broken thair lines & past on but dident know wheather I could brake the seconed or not & put them to flight like I had the first. now before goinge enny father I give you a discription of the road, the first road I started on & the road I come on now come to gather at the edge of jumper town in a shape of letter Ve. the town is just a small town strung out on a ridge. just as I come

46

up to those roads that come to gather thair i seene the dust raising & I remarked to my self the hole reble armmie I guess, but too menny for

-page 9-

one man to tackle so I put on all the brass I had & by them I flew with revolver in hand. I sene thay ware in a hurry or other words somthing had hapened them. they ware goinge down this road that I tride to come, first it was stragler after stragler. I past but know one undertook to halt me & it was a fine thing thay dident for I was more than reckless. I began to think I could lick the hole rebble armie my self.

But now come the tug of war. whare was Co. A. Could I stop & ask the jonnies whare them yanks was & if I was to run into them when on a move thay would fire on me. I sene a bondfire futher on & to my left close too a house I hollered a young fellow stuck his head aroud the corner of the house. Whare in hell is that yankey company I remarked. Right strait a head on that road thar down on the bottom at the foot of the big hill. I turned my horse into the road & let him wak along & was keeping my eyes pealed. finely, I started down the hill, about half way down I was halted. I answered is that you Co. A. the answer come yes. hoo are you? Hensal, I hurd Capton Ritt [*probably Captain Levi H. Utt or perhaps 1ˢᵗ Lt. Aaron M. Pitts*], the man I was caring the dispatch to remark. my god that is company B, but it was onley jim goinge down this hill. when the boyes haulted me thay sene three rebles run right a cross the road in frunt of me. I couldent se down the hill for it was shaded but thay could se up.

47

-page 10-

Capton Ritt remarked it wasent over a quarter of an our when the last shot was fired. When I started the first time thay hurde the rebles & I firing, I was that close to them, but I spoiled thair carculation. thay new whare the company was camped & went up & give them a fight & the boyes whiped tem out.

The Capton swore he couldent see how I got through. he stated that thay had skurmished every foot of the road from wha re this bridge was toren up to whare he went in to camp. I then fetch them back the way I come the last time. How I have this ride about in full. thair is some things I left out.

How a little blow my capton after I maid this ride he remarked to some of his croneys that if he had all such men as jimmie, he wouldent bee afraid to go into the midle of hell. I dont think I would like to bee thair if it is as hot as some say it is. When the reunion was at St. Leouis about 16 yeares ago that was the first time I met enny of the boyes. Co. A. cried my god here is Hensal, do you remember when you saved our lives. thay kised me and huged me. Capton Ritt intended to go back that way if I hadent spoilt their fun in ambush.

Thair is one thing I left out. I am goinge to mension. When I roade up to that revean & tride to cross it & my horse snorted & run back & when those too rebles jumped up in my rear & cocked them shot guns if I ever had a trew sensation of a feeling I

-page 11-

had it. I imagion my hair stood strait on ende. I imagioned I felt my hat rais, but when I got to talking to them fear then left me.

Well, this is all for this time.

Now, General, if you can get a good prompter to corect mistakes & bad spelding & a good tipe riter & one that can sprinkle a little flour on it & then sand paper it off a little & then give it a coat of varnish it may read pretty well.

Youres Truley,

(Signed.) JAMES D.[A.] HENSAL.

General, sir, the way I am situated at presant I cant get away from home, so I scratched this ride my self.

If you can make this out let me know.

The earlier 1869 letter Hensal wrote to General Dodge is one much more grammatical than the one above. In the document containing it General Dodge states:

On March 18, 1869, from Panora, Iowa, J. A. Hensal wrote me as follows:

I noticed in the paper your trip to Atlanta, upon that sacred ground where McPherson fell. [*Major General James Birdseye McPherson was mortally wounded in a skirmish during the Union advance on Atlanta July 22, 1864. He was the highest ranking Union Army commander to die in the Civil War.*][11]

I would like to make a few remarks about that day's battle if it is not out of place. It is still clear before my memory, and it is this. Do you remember of my reporting to you just about the time you gave Sweeney [*Gen. Thomas W. Sweeny*] orders to move out? Beeny Whitehead and I that morning rode out in the direction of Decatur and run across a rebel deserter and he reported about Pardee lying up on that hill and gulch. I hasten in as soon as possible and reprted [*sic*] to you what I had learned. You had just left the troops, and I overhauled you; you were by yourself going in the direction of McPherson's headquarters, when I reported it to you. You made no reply. I then truned [*sic*] and went back, and General Sweeny was just starting and I rode along beside him. Just as we passed that little log hut to our left, you remember, just as we came into the opening there were a few stray shots over in the timber to our lift. The 17th Corps had a hospital just across the hollow and they were moving it. Directly there were more shots fired in that direction, we could see smoke; Sweeney remarked "I wonder what in hell that means." I them told him what I had learned. "The hell, you say; did you report it to Gen. Dodge?" I answered, "Yes" "Where did he go?" I told him you went in the direction of the headquarters. Just about then five or six more shots were fired. The General then turned to me and said "Suppose you ride over in that timber and see what it is." I was riding to the right of the ????ral; I spurred my horses out and made a half left wheel and down the hill I went and across the ravine. I went up in the timber, but not far when my eyes fell upon the three lines of the enemy. I can't see why they did not kill me, but I think I deceived them as I was dressed in butternut. I whirled my horse as quick as lightning, spurred and down into the ravine I went, they then let loose at me. I went on up the hill and, it is useless to state, reported to Gen. Sweeney. They fired about fifty shots at me; they were in plain view of our men before I got up. Our boys fired a volley and so opened that great battle.

THE PAINTING ON THE WINDOW BLIND

Now, General, I have given you the facts in this case; whether you remember my reporting to you or not, I do not know. If Sweeney is living, and you got to see him, and read this to him, I feel positive he will remember it. [*Not likely that Dodge would go see Sweeny since during the Atlanta campaign the two of them got into a fistfight when Dodge broke protocol and personally directed one of Sweeny's brigades. For this confrontation Sweeny was court-martialed but acquitted.*[12]]

I suppose you remember the reunion the next day at Sweeney's quarters. I suppose Fuller [*Gen. John Wallace Fuller*] and Barnes [*Col. James Barnes*] do. Did you ever know that I bantered [*one meaning is "challenged"*] Gen. Fuller for a duel at Decatur, Ala? If Gen. Stephenson [*General Carter L. Stevenson*] is still living, he can tell you all about it as he was an eye witness or his adjutant Armstrong, I think his name was.

Now, General, I suppose you will get tired reading this, as it is poorly written and spelled." [*Signed by James A. Hensal*]

This document was evidently scanned by an OCR and I have tried to correct items I thought were errors created by the character reader—but otherwise made no other changes except for spacing changes.

Additional Information on Hensal's Activities as a Scout

⁓

In addition to these documents originally written by James Hensal, historian William B. Feis sent to me other information relating to Hensal's service as a scout. Dr. Feis said that in his research he had come across Hensal's name, particularly because Hensal had "played an important role in Dodge's intelligence network in Mississippi…" Feis said that Hensal's name appears in various primary sources but less so in secondary sources.

In an e-mail sent to me May 5, 2006 Dr. Feis stated: "I found information on Hensal's scouting activities in Dodge's papers (vouchers for his service and also mentions of him in Dodge's writings) housed at the State Historical Society of Iowa."

Referring to the vouchers: Hensal was paid for the following scouting missions in Mississippi:

"May 25, 1863 to Florence (7 days) $50

June 1, 1863 to Ripley (3 days)

June 3, 1863 to Saltillo (3 days)

June 12, 1863 to Bay Springs (4 days)

June 16, 1863 to LaGrange (2 days)

June 20, 1863 to the gunboats on Tennessee River (3 days)

June 29, 1863 to Cherokee (4 days)

"For each trip in June he was paid $100 and he was injured on
the first trip (June 1)

July 1 to Sept. 1, 1863 for services as "affishant scout and
guide" $150

Sept. 1 to Oct. 31, 1863 for services as scout and guide (61
days) $150

Nov. 1 to Dec. 31 for services as Scout $300."

This list of vouchers shows that Hensal was being paid for
scouting duties commencing in June 1863. It is particularly
interesting because it shows that Hensal was being well paid for his
scouting activities, and it also suggests a major change in his status
as of November 1, 1863. This is about the time he became General
Dodge's chief of scouts, but the exact date of that advancement
remains uncertain and controversial, as we will see later.

Regarding Hensal's pay: Prior to June 1864, a Union private
earned $13 per month. Hensal's salary during July to November
1863 was $75 per month, about three-fourths that of a second
lieutenant. After November 1, 1863, his salary was doubled to
$150, close to that of an infantry major who earned $169 per
month.11F[13] The doubled salary implies a significant upgrade in
Hensal's status, either to Chief of Scouts, or perhaps to Assistant
Chief of Scouts under Levi H. Narin, the man who preceded
Hensal as chief, and was also known as Chickasaw.

That Hensal was serving as General Dodge's chief of scouts
during 1864 is well documented. Part of the documentation consists
of the following communications from Dodge to Hensal contained in
United States War Department, Official Records War of Rebellion,
Series I, volume 32, part 3, Pages 63, 354, and 461. [*These copied by
my father some years ago, and perhaps are not totally accurate.*]

Page 63:

Pulaski, March 13, 1864

Hensal

Chief of Scouts

Send some best men into mountains and make arrangements with Union men living there to go to Rome, Atlanta, Montgomery, and Selma and see what is going on there.

G. M. Dodge
Brigadier-General

*****

Page 354

Athens, April 14, 1864

James Hensal

Chief of Scouts, Decatur:

Do you hear anything from Somerville, Russellville, or Tuscumbia? You must get men out to the rear of Tuscumbia, and see what force is down there. Report fully.

G. M. Dodge
Brigadier-General

*****

Page 461

April 23, 1864

Hensal, Chief of Scouts

Try to get a man out east of Flint to work around in the rear toward Day's Gap, and see what is coming into the valley from that direction.

G. M. Dodge
Brigadier-General

*****

Also contained in General Dodge's archived papers is a letter written April 7, 1864, to General Dodge from Decatur by General Carter L. Stevenson:

"Hensal was within 6 miles of Decatur on the 26th of March. Morgan and his staff left on the 25th, his command moved in advance. They are 7,000 strong and moved north-east. The understanding was that he was going on a grand raid with part of Longstreet's forces. They are to get into our rear either by penetrating our left or turning it. At the same time Forrest is to accomplish the same thing on this flank. He brings a large number of papers, dated as follows: One dated the 2nd of April, they confirm the purpose of the rebels to make damaging raids. John Johnston's entire command is 42,000 infantry, 2,000 artillery and 8,000 cavalry. This the paper strength. Think the effective force is not so large. Nothing from Major Juhn [sp?] as yet."

Also relating to Hensal's Union service are three mostly hand-written documents that I received from Dr. William B. Feis, that were "Reproduced at the National Archives." Here, I reproduce their content. The formal documents are titled "Officer's Certificate of Disability," "General Affidavit," and Neighbor's Affidavit."

The Officer's Certificate of Disability is written by General Grenville Dodge. Underlined words are part of the formal document form, the other words are hand-written:

Des Moines I. Sept 30, 1889.

I, Grenville M. Dodge Brigadier General in command of the left wing of the 16th army corps stationed at Corinth, Miss. certify on honor that James Hensal Private[?] Co B, 7th Kansas was a Scout in my command, and is, as I am informed, an applicant for an Invalid Pension; that he was honorably discharged at the expiration of his term of service in September 1864.

And I further Certify, that the said James Hensal was in the spring of 1863 detailed by me for scout service and was by me sent on a scout to New Albany & Ripley Miss. And in the line of duty on such scout, as reported to me made a charge at Ripley Miss and drove three Rebel companies out of town, and in crossing a Bridge his horse tramped through a hole pitching him forward upon the pommel of the saddle injuring his left testicle. After this time I appointed James Hensal my Chief of Scouts.

And that said, James Hensal, to the best of my knowledge, while serving under me and when he entered the service was of sound, bodily health; but now I consider him as fully entitled to a pension.

Grenville M. Dodge

Later Maj. Gen. U.S.V[?]

The General Affidavit is written by a William Callender of Des Moines, Iowa, age 51, but is undated, states:

"…-James Hensal a member of Co. B. 7th Kansas Vol Cavalry was detached as a scout with me and we received word that James Hensal was sick inside of the rebel line. I was one of the party that was sent in search [of him] and found him at one Dr. Browns (a southern Doctor). Sickness was chronic diarrhoea [sic] and sunstroke from which he layed there about two weeks distant from our lines about 22 miles and I assisted in bringing him inside our lines at

Corinth, Miss. and into our camp. This happened about June 1963. I also remember James Hensal receiving[?] an Injury in a charge made in a raid on Ripley State of Miss. [*words illegible*] often but I think it was in April 1863. Said Injury consisting of a rupture and an enlargement of the tendon on the left of the left testicle."

The Neighbors Affidavit is also written by William Callender on January 14, 1892 [*but it now states his age as 53 instead of 51 as in the previous affidavit*]. It basically states that there was error in the previous affidavit in that Callander was not in the 7th Kansas as implied in the earlier affidavit, but rather was as member of the Second Iowa Infantry, Company D.

William Callender's Other
Writings About James Hensal

⌒⁄⁄⌒

About four years into this continuing investigation I found what appeared to be a newly digitized version of a book by William Callender, *Thrilling Adventures of William Callender, a Union Spy* published by Mills & Company, Printers of Des Moines, Iowa, in 1881. Callender, in early 1861, had joined Company D of the Second Iowa Infantry. He was a scout under the command of General Grenville Dodge, and in this capacity had various associations with Hensal. In his book Callender had this to say about Hensal:

> Having learned that a large Confederate force was encamped somewhere in the vicinity of Ripley, several regiments were sent forward from Corinth to that particular section. I was sent on in front to make a scouting reconnoisance [*sic*], James Hensal, of the Seventh Kansas volunteers, was detailed as my associate. He was a small man, but active and brave as a lion, and his hard service with Jennison, and Jim Lane's far-famed jay-hawkers, had fitted him for any post of severe duty to which he might be assigned.

Callender continued on to describe an adventure the two men had:

We were both well mounted and in good condition for the road. We rode on continuously until we reached the suburbs of Ripley, a town of no very great importance. We halted at a house, dismounted and went in. The first person we saw was an old gentleman seated in a chair in an indolent or suffering attitude, while a colored boy, with brush in hand, was rubbing down his lower limbs. There was something in this which excited Hensal's merriment, and he began to ply the old Southern with seemingly grave but ironical questions. "What is the matter, my friend," said he; "have you got the rheumatism, or is it the gout that is giving you a twitch?"

"Boy is rubbing me for my ease," was the reply. Just then the spirit of mischief seemed to seize Hensal. He drew his revolver in the veriest bravado and flourished it around as though he was going to exterminate everyone within his reach. The terrified boy blanched almost to whiteness, dropped his brush and with a frightened howl, he fled from the room, tumbling heels over head in his rapid exit. For a moment the old citizen was in the direst consternation, fearing that his life would be sacrificed to the fury of this strange assailant. He was stunned by the epithets employed against him, one of which was, and it was a great falsehood, too, that he was disloyal to the South. At length order was restored, and while Hensal was ordering dinner and conversing with one of the women about the house, I took a stroll up town, feeling somewhat ill at ease at the events which had just taken place.

I sauntered leisurely along the street until I came in front of the hotel in the central part of the town. Here I met a citizen with whom I paused to hold a conversation. There were several listeners near by, and as I was a total stranger in the region, though wearing the Confederate garb, I felt assured that I had become an object of suspicion. This thought, together with the fact, perhaps, that the demon of mischief belonging to my friend Hensal had been communicated to me, impelled me to a rash and precipitate act. I was standing with one foot a little elevated when the suspicious circumstances around me began to excite my apprehension, and a remark made by the citizen brought the affair to a crisis. Suddenly, without any premonition, I drew two revolvers from their concealment, and holding one in each hand, commenced firing with remarkable energy, sending the citizen and all other visible listeners to cover. They fled like so many deer started up by the hunters; meanwhile Hensal had just seated himself at the table in the house where our dinner was ordered. He was so intent on satisfying his hunger he did not hear the first shot; but on its frequent repetition his attention was directed to it in a manner so decided that he leaped from his chair, ran out of the house, led forth the horses, one of which he mounted, and hurried to my assistance.

Firing had ceased when he came up, and it seemed we had undisputed possession of the town. Hensal looked grave.

"Bill, you have got us into a scrape, hav'nt [*sic*] you?"

"No: I guess not," I answered; but to tell the truth, I felt quite anxious about consequences. The only way to do, however, was to carry out the programme as we had commenced it—that is, rashly and fearlessly. Leaving the horses for a brief time we rushed into the hotel, with every demonstration of fury, and captured two Confederate soldiers, who had fled thither for refuge. We managed to catch another one outside, and then having executed this exploit, we carried our prisoners to the building in the suburbs where we had first stopped. On the day that these scenes were in progress two companies of rebel soldiers were encamped in the neighborhood of Ripley. So near were they, indeed, that the explosion of my revolver could be heard. Believing that the Yankees were paying a visit to the place their officers ordered them out on double-quick to meet and chastise the cruel invaders. Having some decided intimation of their approach, and resolving to give them a lesson they would not soon forget, we left our three prisoners at the house in the suburbs, informing the owner that we would hold him responsible for their safe-keeping, and stating, also, that if on our return we should fail to find them, we would burn the house over their heads. Much of this was said, doubtless, in bravado, for we hardly had the heart to execute a threat so cruel and vindictive; but the owner accepted it all in dead earnest, and the prisoners declared that their respect for the old citizen and his property would hold them in confinement until we came to take them away.

Having thus disposed of our captives we left the house, remounted our horses and rode with the utmost speed through the village in the direction of the coming Confederates, yelling and firing promiscuously as we rushed past the houses. It so happened that the dust lay to the depth of several inches in the road, and the feet of our horses, as they swiftly sped along, kicked up a cloud of sand and dirt which made all objects in the rear of us, and around us, totally invisible. This dense eclipse, added to the frequent detonations of our revolvers, had the effect to make the approaching enemy believe that they were about to be gobbled up by an army of Yankees a thousand strong, or more. A panic seized them, and instead of advancing on us to give us battle, they wheeled about and fled in fatal confusion.

We pursued them half a mile beyond the limits of the village; then returning in triumph to find our three prisoners where we left them, we chartered a vehicle and conveyed them at once to our command, which was, at the time, about nine miles distant. Thus in that eventful day two Union scouts, without any assistance, except that which nature and our weapons gave us, captured three prisoners, routed two companies of rebels, and held possession of a Confederate town for at least two hours. That was glory enough for one day.

Scout William Callender tells of another daring adventure undertaken with James Hensal:

General Dodge found it convenient to change headquarters from Corinth, Mississippi, to Pulaski, Tennessee. [*The move was on November 2, 1863*[14]] I was sent with Hensal from the latter place to learn all that could be ascertained in relation to a Confederate force reported to have crossed the Tennessee River at or near Lamb's Ferry, some thirty-five miles from Pulaski. We made the trip without finding what we sought, for no rebel troops were seen in that vicinity. Returning, we arrived at Sugar Creek, fifteen miles from headquarters, after nightfall. At this point we rode up to a dwelling, which was inhabited, as we learned a little later, by two Confederate war-widows, and their children. Here we had permission to put up for the night.

After caring for our horses and partaking of supper we were directed to an out-building, a short distance from the residence, where we were to lodge until morning. It was a dark night, and very cold, too, for the season and the latitude. We fastened the door and then building a fire I sat down to enjoy it, while Hensal, who was weary and inclined to slumber, retired to rest. I was morbidly watchful and alert, feeling, for some mysterious reason, I had need of all the vigilance that could be summoned to my aid.

I was still sitting at the fire enjoying the warmth as it was communicated to my chilled frame, when my quick hearing caught the sound of horses' feet approaching the house. Soon after a party of men were heard to dismount and enter the building where the families resided. Cautiously I left my seat, went to Hensal and aroused him, saying in a whisper, "the rebels are after us." My companion started up in a hurry; and then after making due preparation we silently unfastened the door and proceeded out in the dense darkness on a tour of investigation. Stealthily we stepped to a window of the dwelling, from which a pane had been broken out, and through which a sickly light was gleaming from an antiquated saucer lamp. From our post of observation we saw, with more or less distinctness, five Confederate officers, all of them being commissioned, as the symbols they wore indicated. They were seated around the room, seemingly delighted to find a temporary refuge from the cold and darkness.

Having seen all we desired, and much more than we had bargained for, we retired from the window to hold a brief consultation. It was agreed between us that Hensal should proceed to the front door, and I should return to the window. Our object was to capture, by stratagem, this whole rebel delegation. We posted ourselves according to arrangement and waited for a favorable opportunity to execute our plan. By accident the door was a little ajar; and one of the women, standing near it, caught a glimpse of my friend on the outside. The silent start she made was not observed by any one; for an officer, just at the time, attracted attention to himself by remarking, "this is a very cold night, indeed."

The time had now come for action; and the voice of Hensal rang out on the night like the blast of a trumpet— "Come out here and I'll make it d—d hot for you."

The officers, taken thus by storm, started up in dismay and moved backward from the door toward the window through which I was gazing. It was my time now to address the beleaguered garrison—

"Confound you," I exclaimed, "I'll make it hot for you *here*."

This was the nearest approach to profanity I ever made in my scouting experience. Simultaneously, or as nearly so as the nature of the case permitted, we commanded every man in the room to hold up his hands or suffer death; and while they all did so with alacrity we issued our orders to an imaginary troop of Union soldiers around us, assigning to different ones their part of duty in this emergency. As nothing could be seen on the exterior, owing to the profound darkness, our ruse had the desired effect. The enemy believed that the house was surrounded on all sides by a formidable Yankee host, and they felt that resistance was useless. [*It seems odd that Callender considered "confound you" to be profane, but in those days it was different. Attesting to that was the formation of the Anti-Profanity Association in Panora in 1870 by 45 men, one perhaps being James Hensal. The group wanted to ban all expressions involving the name of the Diety plus other expressions such as darned, darn, darn it, dermit, holy cats, by George, dog gon it, and by jingo.*[15]]

Hensal at the door ordered them to come out one at a time; and the first one who approached was met by an authoritative command to stand aside in silence, while I, who meantime had retired from the window, disarmed him of all deadly weapons. One after another of these rebel dignitaries came out to give themselves up unconditionally; and when the last man had passed through the mortifying ordeal we conducted the whole five to the building where we had designed to sleep during the night. There we fastened them in, while we remained outside to watch.

It was not until morning that the officers, or the ladies, discovered that the important capture had been accomplished alone through the personal agency of two Union soldiers. The humiliation of the men was bitter and intense; and it was diminished in no respect, when, under cover of our revolvers, we compelled them to mount their horses and take the road in front of us to Pulaski, where we turned them over to the proper authorities. A sorry, crest-fallen set they were, who never forgot the bitter lesson which was taught them on this occasion.

These two little stories tell much about Hensal's and Callender's impetuous, devil-may-care approach to their spying activities. It also says something about the nature of the work they were performing. In principle, the primary role of the scout was to uncover information about the disposition of enemy forces and the intent of the enemy commanders, but if that effort involved a bit of hell-raising and direct fighting, that was fine, too. Although part of the Union army, they were free to act on their own initiative. At one point in his book (page 17) Callender comments directly on this matter:

> [*As a scout*] I was now entering on the performance of duties of the most thrilling and dangerous character, yet, nevertheless, there was a fascination about them which strongly invited rather than repelled adventure. In all military enterprises there is constant danger, but the army scout, occupying as he does a position outside of the general military system, literally takes his life in his own hands. If he be captured by the enemy he may expect no quarter. From time immemorial the laws of war have consigned the captured spy and scout to a prompt and ignominious death.

A historian's take on the role of Union scouts comes from William B. Feis, author of a recently published article entitled "That great essential of success, Espionage, Covert Action, and Military Intelligence"[16] (As a frontispiece to his article Dr. Feis presents, with my permission, the Hood painting of Hensal, and he refers to Hensal as well.) Dr. Feis describes the role of Union scouts as follows:

> Mostly volunteers from the ranks, scouts performed a variety of missions. Typically, a scout patrolled along enemy lines but at times, either in civilian garb or a Confederate uniform, penetrated hostile territory to get a better look. Operating alone or in organized units, scouts sought information on enemy movements, deployments, order of battle, and terrain but at times they also hunted guerrillas. In all these pursuits, operatives flirted with extreme danger. Perhaps reflecting the thoughts of many fellow scouts, James Hensal, who survived at least seven missions behind enemy lines, wrote later that when ordered to carry a dispatch into enemy territory, he always knew that "if I got through it would bee [*sic*] a merical [*sic*]."

How James Hensal Became a Spy

⁓

As mentioned earlier, the family lore regarding James Hensal contains the telling of an intriguing incident involving him, one so odd and initially without substantiation that right from the start of this investigation I and others questioned if it ever happened. Five years later as I complete this document I can now state that the incident did actually occur, but almost certainly not in the way told in the family story. I now have uncovered in the literature two other versions of the story, each differing from the other, and even more so from the family lore version. However, the three accounts each contain a description of the essential incident about which the story revolves: the fact that James Hensal shot and killed his superior officer Captain Fred Swoyer, and for the act was court-martialed and sentenced to death. The execution was never carried out.

I now recite the three versions of the story, and I note beforehand that the differences between the three versions illustrate how much distortion can occur by both the viewpoints of those telling a story and by subsequent retellings coupled with vagaries of memory.

The family lore version of the story comes from notes made by my father Bon V. Davis in the late 1960s when he visited Iowa and became interested in the history of James A. Hensal. It contains the essence of the story but certain elements of it are almost certainly untrue. According to this version, James Hensal was standing in rank at the command of his superior office Captain Fred Swoyer. Swoyer often imbided and tended to be vicious when drunk, as he was on this particular day. Captain Swoyer ordered the man standing next to Hensal to straighten up. The man could not do as ordered because he was a hunchback and so Swoyer shot him, whereupon Hensal shot and killed Swoyer. Hensal was court-martialed and sentenced to be shot once President Abraham Lincoln had signed the execution order. At the time, the execution of any Union soldier required the president's approval. Lincoln approved, and the night before Hensal was to be shot at sunrise, he was being held in a tent on a hilltop. He was sick and unable to walk. During the night, fellow soldiers crept up the hill, split open the back of the tent and made off with Hensal. The unit was on march and so the soldiers carried Hensal along outside the line of march until he was well enough to navigate on his own. He then ran off and later joined another regiment.

If this incident were to have happened as reported here I thought when I began this investigation that it had to have taken place early in the war, perhaps about the time of the formation of the Kansas 7th regiment in late 1861. But that idea did not jibe with the fact that Captain Swoyer was still around during 1862—unless the officer Hensal shot actually was some other man. The official record states that Captain Swoyer was "killed in action" at Somerville, Tennessee, on January 3, 1863.

The second version of the story about Hensal doing in Swoyer comes from the *Tennessee Civil War Sourcebook, January 1863*[17] which contains documents written by participants and listed day-by-day. Among the entries for January 3, 1863, are two that refer to Swoyer's death, making it clear that while the official record states that he was "killed in action," he was actually killed by his own men. One entry is by Col. A. L. Lee who was commanding a brigade consisting of the Kansas Seventh Cavalry and ten companies of the Illinois Fourth Cavalry.

On January 2, 1863, Col Lee received orders from General Grant and Brig. Gen. C. S. Hamilton, commander of the Union's District of West Tennessee, to collect as many horses, mules, saddles, and bridles as possible in preparation for actions to take place between Hatchie and Tallahatchie. In response, Col. Lee detached companies from his column to search for the requested animals and equipment, and then at 7 p. m. bivouacked at a plantation 6 miles from Somerville. During the following miserable night Lee's men, without supper and in the rain, moved against suspected Confederate forces at Somerville. They found none, but were happy that, as Lee stated:

> The people of the town treated the soldiers well, and offered them in singular profusion wines and liquors of all kinds. The town was literally full of intoxicating liquors. At one store-house I discovered fourteen barrels of whisky which belonged to the Confederate Army. As a result of this unfortunate profusion of strong drinks, many soldiers, who had neither supper nor breakfast, and laid on the ground without shelter, through a night of pelting storm, were induced to drink, and as a consequence I suddenly discovered that many were intoxicated.
>
> Here occurred a melancholy incident. At the southern border of the town, Company B, of the Seventh Kansas, Capt. Fred. Swoyer, had been stationed as a picket. The

captain had discovered a quantity of commissary stores in a building near, and stationed a guard at the entrance. The captain himself had visited a house near by [*sic*] to obtain a breakfast, and there drank to such an extent as to become somewhat exhilarated. During his absence, a couple of men of his company persisted in an endeavor to pass into the store-house mentioned, but were prevented by the guard. On his return to his company the case was reported.

He directed the company to fall in, and the men alluded to deliver their arms and go in arrest. His tone was harsh and peremptory in the extreme. One of the men demurred, and attempted to explain. He commanded him to desist and remove his arms, drawing his pistol, and telling him he would shoot him if he said another word. The man again spoke, when the captain fired, the ball passing into the body of the man. Instantly one of the company fired at the captain, but did not wound him. The captain rode toward him and the man ran. The captain soon overtook him, both riding rapidly, and shot him through the head, killing him instantly. At the same moment the man fired, and his ball passed through the body of the captain. The company was in confusion, and many shots were fired at the captain, who rode rapidly into town. He was taken into a house and died the following day.

During this occurrence I was at the court-house, a half mile from its scene. I immediately dispatched the commanding officer of the regiment with a company to quell the mutiny. It was readily quieted, though the men remained much excited.

In the following portion of his report Col. Lee demonstrates his awareness that no good might come of this incident, and so wrote what he could to minimize the damage.

That night we bivouacked south of Wolf River, near Moscow, and next morning reached our camp, bringing with us nearly 300 head of captured mules and horses.

At Somerville two or three stores were opened and some plundering effected by drunken men. From complaints made and proven to me, I have no doubt, too, that robbery and outrages were committed by drunken men. No plunder of goods, however, was made to any considerable extent, as nothing that could be seen was carried by soldiers from town.

The officers of the command were sober, and did all in their power to enforce order among the men. My personal staff especially risked their lives in quelling insubordination of drunken men.

Arriving at camp, I directed regimental courts-martial, to try all men who had become intoxicated. This was done, and the next day the command was paraded, and sentences of the courts, depriving more than 200 of one month's pay, and inflicting further punishments, were published.

At my request, a general court-martial was immediately called to try the graver offenses, which has continued to session till a recent date. Regarding this unfortunate expedition, I can only say, in mitigation of its excesses, for more than a month immediately preceding these troops had been engaged in the most arduous, dangerous, and fatiguing service, and during most of that time had subsisted alone on what could be gleaned from the country. They were almost worn out. The absence of two successive meals, and the suffering incident to the severe exposure of the night previous, induced them readily to drink, and the liquor was necessarily speedy in its effects. Before any one [*sic*] could suspect the possibility of such an event, numbers were drunk.

In our campaigns we have, with this single exception, never found in country or town intoxicating drinks. Its present scarcity in the South is proverbial; hence no special precautions suggested themselves to prevent inebriety.

I am, captain, your obedient servant,

A. L. LEE, Col., Cmdg. Second Brigade, Cavalry Division.

(Here there is reference to *OR*, Ser. I, Vol. 24, pt. III, pp. 142-143.)

However Col Lee's excuses did not cut it with General Grant. In a message to Brig. Gen. C. S. Hamilton on January 20, 1863, Grant wrote[18]:

Complaints have come in from Somerville from the few Union men of the outrageous conduct of the Seventh Kansas, and in one case of Col. Lee's conduct where he was informed of the status of the party. This was the case of Mr. Rivers, who called on Col. Lee to try and get him to restrain his men, and was replied to by being made to dismount and give up the animal he was riding.

If there are any further complaints, well substantiated, I wish you to arrest Col. Lee and have him tried for incompetency and his regiment dismounted and disarmed.

The conduct of this regiment at New Albany, in their pursuit of Van Dorn, stopping to plunder the citizens instead of pursuing the enemy when they were so near them, and again when after Richardson, about the 8th of this month, they passed near where they knew or at least were informed he was and went on to the town for the purpose of plunder-all the laurels won by the regiment and their commander on the pursuit of the enemy from Holly Springs to Coffeeville have been more than counterbalanced by their bad conduct since.

Their present course may serve to frighten women and children and helpless old men, but will never drive out an armed enemy.

I am, general, with great respect, yours, &c.

U. S. GRANT, Maj.-Gen.

(Here there is reference to *OR*, Ser. I, Vol. 17, pt. II, p. 575.)

Another account of the shooting of Captain Swoyer comes from a member of the 7th Kansas Cavalry, listed as the [*Fletcher*] Pomeroy diaries, January 3, 1863.[19]

Near Moscow, Tenn., Saturday, Jan. 3, 1863-We were called out at 3:00 A. M. without the sound of bugle or loud orders and were not allowed any fires or lights. It began raining about that time. We moved out at 4.30 A. M. and reached Somerville, five mi[l]es distant, soon after daylight. We surrounded it and posted pickets on every road. The town was searched. 175 horses and mules were found, and a large number of arms and several prisoners. A large amount of liquor was also found, and as the men were cold and hungry, many of them embibed [*sic*] more or less and became intoxicated. Company "B" became quite disorderly, and in trying to quell them, Capt. Sawyer [*Swoyer*] killed one man and severely wounded another, and then was fatally shot, himself, by his men. This compelled Col. Lee to retire from the place. We left town about noon. It rained hard nearly all the forenoon. We marched twelve miles and are bivouacked in the woods. It is raining hard and we have no shelter.

—Pomeroy Diaries, January 3, 1863. [*The roster of Company D of the Kansas 7th Cavalry lists Private Fletcher Pomeroy from Wyanet, Ill.; also Emerson W. Pomeroy of the same town.*]

These two accounts of the events of January 3, 1863, do not mention James Hensal by name, but they verify that while drunk Captain Fred Swoyer shot one or two of his men being placed in formation and then was killed by his own men. General Grant was so furious at what had taken place at Somerville that he later threatened not only to remove Col. Lee from command but also to disband the whole outfit. The event certainly strengthened Company B's reputation as a bunch of miscreants.

Finally we come to the third version of the story, one I had not been aware of until August 2010, some five years into this investigation. It comes second-hand from James Hensal himself, and probably is the most accurate. It also explains how Hensal, at least formally, got into the scouting business.

Before reciting this version of the story I refer back to the letter James Hensal wrote to General Grenville Dodge in 1907.

This letter describes an event that most likely occurred near the end of 1862, about three months before the death of Capt. Fred Swoyer. (I had previously assumed that the letter described an event occurring during Hensal's tenure as a scout, but now that seems not to be the case.)

In the letter, Hensal states that after the battle of Corinth (fought October 3-4, 1862) the Kansas 7th Cavalry's Companies A and B were ordered to Rienzi for scouting duties. When the order came Company A was out on a scout, and so there was need to send someone out to call them in. According to Hensal's letter, when Captain Fred Swoyer received refusals from four other men "he then called the boy jimmie as he always called me. now this was the first duty he required of me sinse he laid his shoulder straps for me." From this statement it appears that Hensal had done something to irritate Captain Swoyer and that he had then beaten Hensal with his shoulder straps. Perhaps that act contributed to what would happen to Swoyer on January 3, 1863.

In this long letter Hensal tells of his dangerous ride through scattered enemy forces to search for Company A. That ride may have initiated Hensal's reputation for fearlessness and bravery, or merely added to it. That ride might also have been instrumental in his being picked by General Dodge for a subsequent mission that would lead to Hensal later becoming designated as a scout under General Dodge.

This third version of the story is contained in the *Guthrie Center Guthrian* on August 29, 1901, a newspaper published in Guthrie Center, a town some six miles west of Panora, Iowa. The article starts out by reprinting another short one that had appeared in the *Perry Daily Chief,* published in Perry, a town approximately 15 miles northeast of Panora. Titled "Reflections," the article exhibits the sometimes gossipy nature of small-town newspaper writing of the time. The full text follows:

James Hensal, a prosperous farmer living near Panora, was in Perry a few days ago, for the first time in many years. Mr. Hensal used to market his grain and other farm products in Perry in the days when this was the nearest railroad town. His visit here the other day recalled many pleasant incidents of those early days. Not many of the merchants who were in active business life in Perry in the early seventies are now to be found. W.H. Chandler of whom Mr. Hensal bought his farm machinery, was out of town the other day, a fact very much regretted by the visitor, who had a great deal to say about "Chans" honorable dealings. Bob Ginn, the pioneer grain dealer, was here however, and the two old neighbors had an enjoyable talk about old times. Mr. Hensal was a famous scout during the war of the rebellion and a life long friend of Gen. Dodge, under whom he served. In fact the friendship between the commander and his famous chief of scouts has grown stronger as the years have gone by Gen. Dodge, now a prominent New York railroad magnate, and reputed to be many times a millionaire, is always glad to see "Jim" Hensal, who more than once took his life in his hands to save his chief [*a gross exaggeration no doubt, unless the reporter meant to use the word "serve" rather than "save"*] Said a Perry soldier who knew him well "If all the soldiers of the Union ranks had been as brave as Hensal the war would not have lasted so long. That fellow had no idea of what fear meant." Mr. Hensal is an honored citizen of the community in which he lives. His Perry friends will be glad to see him again and often. —*Perry Chief Reporter*

The above reminds us of an incident in the life of James Hensal which was related to us the past summer. While at our home in Upper Sandusky, Ohio, we called to see our old friend George Kenan, a druggist of that city and a veteran of the civil war. Under the influence of a fragrant cigar he became reminiscent and remarked to us, "You know Jim Hensal of your county", [sic] Upon our replying that we knew Jim, he said, "Jim Hensal was a brave a man as ever fired a shot. He and I belonged to the same regiment, the 7th Kansas Cavalry, commonly called the 'Kansas Jayhawkers'. [*The official record states that George Kenan was in Company A; see roster listing presented earlier.*] Our captain was a brave man but totally irresponsible when under the influence of liquor, and he was frequently in that condition, and had often threatened to shoot some of the boys of the company for the least infraction of his orders. One day after they had captured and looted a small town the captain became drunk and ugly. He ordered his company to fall in, but one young Irishman did not 'dress up' with the line for the reason that he was somewhat intoxicated. To the drunken captain this was a disobedience of orders that demanded summary punishment and thereupon he pulled a revolver from his holster and shot him dead. Quick as a flash three shots from the company followed and the captain rolled from the saddle, a dead man. Hensal and two companions were immediately taken in custody and tried, by court martial. Hensal was condemned to be shot and the proceedings were sent to Washington to be signed by President Lincoln. During this time Hensal was kept in the guard house under guard pending the return of his sentence from Washington. One night Gen. Dodge had occasion to send a man upon an important and perilous mission. He sent for Hensal and said to him 'I have a duty that I want you to perform. You are now the same as a dead man. You may be killed, as the undertaking is a hazardous one. If you escape and return in safety, I may be able to avert the doom now hanging over your head.' Hensal accepted the terms stipulating that he was to have a certain horse to ride, which was furnished to him. He was only a beardless boy of nineteen, but a fearless horseman, a crack shot, and as he rode away from the headquarters that night, none ever expected to again see him alive. [*Actually, Hensal was twenty-five, not nineteen.*] His acquaintance with the locality, his superb horsemanship and daring carried him through the dangers of the night, and he safely delivered the dispatches consigned to his care. On his return he was given other duties and he became a trusted and valued scout at the headquarters of both Gen. Dodge and Gen. Sherman. Upon return of the death sentence signed by President Lincoln, Gen. Sherman remarked in his sententious way that he supposed the president thought the rebels were not killing enough good men and wanted him to take a hand in it. He turned the document over to Gen. Dodge who carefully laid it aside. Hensal rose to the position of chief scouts and at the close of the war he was taken by Gen. Dodge to Washington before the Secretary of war, E. M. Stanton, who reinstated him on the rolls, and then the document that sentenced him to death was destroyed." As we rose to separate for the night Mr. Kenan said to us, "I tell you it is an honor to know Jim Hensal. A braver man never fired a shot for the preservation of the Union, and your county in Iowa should be proud of the fact that you have him for a citizen." Mr. Kenan also informed us that Col. Cody of Wild West fame was also a member of that regiment, but unlike Hensal, won his fame after the civil war. [*The official record agrees with this last statement of Kenan's.*]

So there is little doubt that that James Hensal actually did kill his superior officer Captain Fred Swoyer, but that the family lore version of the story is highly distorted and lacking in detail. The second and third versions are compatible, and together provide much more information about the incident. They differ slightly in detail but essentially tell the same story, and because of that and partial verification through documentation developed near the time of occurrence, these two have the ring of truth.

In summary, we can be quite certain that this incident occurred on January 3, 1863 at Somerville, Tennessee. Captain Fred Swoyer was in command of part or all of a force that included members of Companies A and B of the Kansas 7th Cavalry that entered Somerville intending to move against suspected Confederate forces and collect horses and related equipment. The troops found no significant enemy force but did collect horses, mules, related equipment, arms and a few prisoners. They also found much liquor which many of the men, including Capt. Swoyer, consumed and became intoxicated. At one point Capt. Swoyer, mounted on horseback, ordered the men to fall in but one man, probably Private Timothy Mullen of Company A failed to do so to Swoyer's satisfaction and so Swoyer shot him with a pistol, killing Mullen. Whereupon Hensal and perhaps other soldiers shot Swoyer who either died immediately or soon thereafter. One witness on the scene, Private Fletcher Pomeroy of Company D wrote an account of the incident in his diary, and another, Private W. George Kenan of Company A related his account to a newspaper reporter many years later, both accounts being in substantial agreement. Brigade commanding officer Col A. L. Lee, located one-half mile from the scene of the action, wrote a contemporary report that differed somewhat in detail but largely confirmed the other two accounts.

Col. Lee convened regimental courts-martial that took away two months pay from more than 200 men who had overly imbibed at Somerville. He also convened a general court-martial which sentenced Hensal to death. While awaiting the required approval of the death warrant by President Lincoln (or by secretary of war E. M. Stanton) Hensal was placed under guard. According to Kenan's account, the approved warrant came back to General Sherman who gave it to General Dodge. However in the meantime, General Dodge called James Hensal in and asked him to go on a scouting mission that he probably would not survive. Hensal did survive, and so General Dodge laid the warrant aside and allowed Hensal to go on other missions which he performed so well that Dodge later appointed him chief of scouts.

This event much embarrassed the officers of the Union army, as is shown by Col. Lee's attempt to excuse the actions of his men at Somerville, and General Ulysses Grant's response. Grant was so furious over the incident that he threatened to try Col. Lee for incompetency and also to dismount and disarm his regiment. Then according to the account of Private Kenan recited long after the war, Secretary of War E. M. Stanton later destroyed one important record of the event: Hensal's death warrant signed by President Lincoln.

In the grand scheme of things, Hensal's shooting of Swoyer was not a significant event of the Civil War, but it certainly did influence the futures of the two men involved. It terminated Swoyer's life and was apparently crucial to Hensal's becoming a scout and his later rise to become chief of scouts for General Dodge. Most of those hearing of the event—and surely many of his fellow soldiers in the 7th Kansas Cavalry did—probably considered Hensal's shooting of Swoyer as justified, but not something to be talked about officially. Illustrating that idea is a passage in a speech given December 2, 1902 to the 27th annual meeting of the Kansas State Historical Society by Adjutant General Simeon M. Fox.[20] In his speech he made many laudatory remarks about various officers of the 7th Kansas Cavalry. Of Capt. Fred Swoyer, he said, "Captain Swoyer was a man of great physical courage, but exceedingly reckless [*meaning when under the influence*]. In the winter of 1861-62 he did a little steeple-chasing down Delaware street, in Leavenworth, and while putting his horse over a sleigh loaded with cordwood, standing across the street, the animal fell and broke the captain's leg. He limped through the rest of his life. His death was the result of his recklessness, but he was brave and patriotic and did splendid service while he lived."

It was best not to talk too much about what actually happened that night of January 3, 1863, at Somerville, but James Hensal was soon to be involved in another event that received much more attention, and from those on both sides of the Civil War conflict. This was the capture and execution of Confederate spy Sam Davis. That story has special relevance here because it relates to the date on which Hensal became chief of scouts. As with Hensal's shooting of Swoyer, the details of that event were puzzling right from the start of this investigation into the background of Hood's painting of Hensal.

The Capture of Sam Davis, Boy Hero of the South

⟨❦⟩

Hensal's role as a spy and later becoming General Dodge's chief of scouts is well documented. However, an interesting issue centers around the exact date he became chief, mainly because it affects our understanding of the role played by Hensal in a famous event of November 1863, the capture and execution of the "Boy Hero of the South" Sam Davis.

It would seem that there is little to debate about the matter if the writings of General Dodge are to be taken at face value. One of his statements defines Hensal's dates of service:

"One very valuable spy was James Hensal of the 7th Kansas, now Iowa. He was my chief of scouts October 1863 to August 1864. He often went inside the enemy's lines and performed very valuable services. I think he was the most daring and fearless young fellow I ever saw."

Another of General Dodge's statements specifically states that James Hensal captured Sam Davis:

"We had hardly gotten settled when the enemy's guerillas and scouts inside our lines commenced their depredations. I had with me a very bright young man as chief of my scouts, James Hensal of the 7th Kansas and I detailed several men who had been on these duties and turned them over to him. The first capture he made was a very important one. It included Sam Davis, [*and*] Capt. Shaw, who then was Capt. Coleman who was the head of the Coleman scouts operating within my line."

Also suggesting Hensal's direct involvement and that he was chief of scouts at the time is a statement in the *Tennessee Historical Quarterly, Volume XXIV,* page 305):

"On Friday, November 20 after spending the night at his home, he [*Sam Davis*] made his way through Union lines with dispatches for Gen. Bragg. He was halted by a man who told him that he was 'conscripting' him for the Confederacy. Under this pretense he, Private R. S. King, took Sam's arms, then placed him under arrest. Private R. S. King was under Chief Scout Hensal."

However, these passages are only part of the written record, and other documents suggest that Levi H. Narin, Hensal's predecessor as chief of scouts, actually captured Sam Davis. Before going into that issue, it seems fitting to tell more about what happened to Sam Davis to make him such a heroic figure.

A much heralded incident of the Civil War was the capture and hanging of the "Boy Hero of the Confederacy" Sam Davis in late November 1863. The essence of the dramatic story of Sam Davis is contained in the wording of a plaque placed beside a monument at the site of his capture, both shown in the accompanying photograph. The plaque reads:

Born Oct. 6, 1842
Enlisted April 30, 1861
captured Nov 19, 1863
Executed Nov 27, 1863

A young Confederate soldier better known as Sam Davis from Smyrna, Tenn. was a private in the 1st Tenn. Infantry. He was 19 years old & was a scout under Capt. Coleman, alias Dr. H. B. Shaw, Known as Coleman's Scouts. Coleman's Scouts were gathering information about the union forces moving from Middle Tenn.

On Nov 20, [sic] 1863, Davis was captured by the Seventh Kansas Calvary on Lambs Ferry Road just below Minor Hill. He was carrying improtant [sic] documents to General Braxton Bragg in Chattanooga. Davis was carried to Pulaski, Tenn. where he was jailed. He was court marshaled & condemned to death by hanging. General Dodge offered Davis his freedom for the source of his information. Davis refused to tell repeatedly. The 21- year old soldier proclaimed! "NO, I CANNOT, I WOULD RATHER DIE A THOUSAND DEATHS THAN BETRAY A FRIEND OR BE FALSE TO A DUTY."

On the eve of his execution he wrote his Mother a letter.

Dear Mother, Oh how painful it is to write to you. I have to die Tomorrow morning – to be hung fy [sic] the Federals. Mother do not grieve fo [sic] me. I must bid you good-bye forever more, Mother. I do not hate to die.

Give my love to all.   Your Dear Son Sam

On Nov 27, 1863 Davis rode in a wagon, seated upon his own coffin From Giles County jail to a hill in East Pulaski overlooking the town. This was where the 21-year [old] hero was hung to death. Sam Davis was buried in Pulaski at Maplewood Cemetery, a few days later, a friend of the family & a younger brother rode into Pulaski in a wagon to identify the body. They exhumed the body, which was identified as Davis & then carried back to Smyrna, Tenn. Where his Mother was hoping to see an empty wagon return but instead it was carrying her son's body. He was buried Christmas Eve in the family cemetery.

Below the encircled D on the top of the monument itself are the words:

PLACE WHERE SAM DAVIS WAS CAPTURED NOV.19, 1863 MINOR HILL, TENN. WHEN OFFERED HIS FREEDOM FOR INFORMATION, HIS ANSWER WAS "NO, I CANNOT, I WOULD RATHER DIE A THOUSAND DEATHS THAN BETRAY A FRIEND OR BE FALSE TO A DUTY." NO GREATER LOVE HATH MAN THAN THIS, LIFE FOR ONE'S FRIEND TO GIVE THAT SOUL DIVINE, SPEAKS TO HIS FOE, "I DIE THAT YOU MAY LIVE."

Monument to Sam Davis at Minor Hill, Tennessee, the site of his capture. (Photographed October 2006.)

It is clear that the wording of the plaque and memorial shown in the photographs contain some errors. There are numerous accounts of the Sam Davis affair in archival material and the published literature, and most state that the date of his capture was November 20, 1863, not November 19, as stated on the memorials. Neither the plaque (with its several errors) nor the monument mention the startling fact that, during the week of Davis' imprisonment, the man General Dodge's troops were really after, Captain E. Coleman, alias Captain Henry B. Shaw, was also captured and was lodged in a cell next to the one holding Sam Davis. He was Davis' immediate commanding officer, and the one Davis was protecting. Davis reportedly was the youngest soldier to receive the Confederate Medal of Honor, and his story became a rallying point for the southern cause in the waning days of the Confederacy.

The many accounts of the Sam Davis capture in archival material and the published literature differ in detail but the essence of the story is as given here.

Sam Davis Museum and plaque at Pulaski, Tennessee, erected on the site of his execution. (Photographed October 2006.)

Monument to Sam Davis erected in the town square at Pulaski, Tennessee. (Photographed October 2006.)

Contrasting Claims

⌒✳⌒

Contrasting with the previous statements that Hensal was then chief of scouts and it was his men who captured Sam Davis is the contention by Levi H. Naron that in late November 1863, *he* was chief of scouts and that it was *his* men who had captured Sam Davis. These claims come from the book *Chickasaw, a Mississippi Scout for the Union* written by R. W. Surby, and originally published as part of another book in 1865. Surby stated that Naron dictated to him the material in the original book relating to Naron. Material quoted here is from an edition of the book edited by Thomas D. Cockrell and Michael B. Ballard and published by the Louisiana State University Press, Baton Rouge, 2005. Even the edited version of the book contains errors; the few pages I have examined in detail contained several misspellings of peoples' names and one misidentification: 1) On page 131 the man identified as Rhoddy, the former commander of the 4th Alabama Cavalry was actually P. D. Roddey. 2) The footnote on page 131 erroneously suggests that the Lieut. Col. Johnson identified in the text was probably Armory K. Johnson, but other sources indicate that he was Col. William A. Johnson.[21] 3) On page 132, in two places, Hensal is wrongly spelled Hansel.

On Pages 127-28 of Surby's book , Narin says:

A few days after the above occurrence, I sent out two of my scouts dressed in Confederate uniforms. While on return to their camp they met a young man dressed in rebel uniform, whom they conscripted for the rebel army [*This was the capture of Sam Davis.*] The young man was very indignant at first, and told them that they were doing wrong, that he was on special business from General Bragg, all of which was to no avail; my scouts persisted in taking him before their Captain, who could act at his pleasure…. {Editors' Footnote: the captain of scouts was Captain W. F. Armstrong, General Dodge's provost marshal.} He was taken to headquarters [*where they found various incriminating papers on Davis*]….The General [*Dodge*] then turned him over to me, with orders to deliver him to the Provost Marshal and to have him put in a cell, also, to tell him that he had only a few days to live; except on one condition would his life be spared, that was, to tell who the person was that furnished him with those papers. He replied that he would not confess anything. {Editors' Footnote: Braxton Bragg's chief of scouts in Middle Tennessee was Captain Henry B. Shaw, whose operative name was E. Coleman. He was in custody at the same time as Davis, which was one of the reasons Davis refused to talk….}….The next day a commission was called to give him a trial. The prisoner was called out, who confessed to the charge preferred against him. He was sentenced to be hung on the following Friday. When he was taken to the scaffold I was permitted to talk with him. I addressed him thus: "Davis, you are not the man that should be hung, and if you will tell me who General Bragg's chief of scouts was so I might capture him, your life would yet be spared." He looked me steadily in the eye, and said[,] "[D]o you suppose were I your friend that I would betray you?" I told him I did not know, but life was sweet to all men. His reply to this, was, "sir if you think I am that kind of man you have missed your mark. You may hang me a thousand times and I would not betray my friends." I then left him, only to witness in less than two minutes afterwards his fall from the scaffold, a dead man. Thus ended the life of Sam Davis....

Narin states on page 101 of the biography:

"I soon decided to report myself at Corinth. Arriving at the latter place the next day [*Feb 16, 1863*] and immediately reporting myself to General Dodge, who requested me to take charge of his scouts. On seeing them I at first declined; they were not the kind of men for the business. I told the General if he had anything that myself or my friend Bennett could perform, that all he had to do was to command and we would undertake the job ourselves without the assistance of others."

However, within the same paragraph is a contradicting statement in which Narin then tells of sending out men to perform certain scouting duties. Also in contradiction regarding the dates of Narin's service as chief of scouts is, on page 170, a copy of a letter from General Dodge to R. W. Surby, apparently written about 1865 when the account was published. One sentence states, "L, H. Narin ("Chickasaw") was in my employ as Chief of Scouts, and secret service corps, for more than a year."

If, as Narin says, he became chief of scouts in February 1863 and if he served for more than a year in that capacity, as the letter from General Dodge claims, then Narin was chief of scouts in November when Davis was captured. Yet that does not jibe with material contained on pages 131-32 of the biography. There, Narin tells about his being wounded near Lamb's Ferry shortly after the capture of Sam Davis:

> One rebel stood beside the road and, as I came up, leveled his revolver within two inches of my head and fired, the ball just grazing my neck, and the powder burning my face and singeing my hair...My wound was not of serious nature....My wound now began to trouble me, and I applied to the General for a leave of absence, to visit my family up North. I now felt that I had had my fill of satisfaction. The following is a correct copy of the Special Order relieving me from duty for a certain time:

> HEADQUARTERS LEFT-WING SIXTEENTH ARMY CORPS, PULASKI, TENNESSEE. Dec 15, 1863.
> SPECIAL ORDER,
> No. 39.
> VI. L. H. N----[*Narin*], in employ of United States Government, is hereby ordered to Illinois, on business for this command. The Q.M. Department will furnish transportation. He will turn over his quartermaster and ordinance stores to James Hensel [*Hensal*], taking proper

receipts therefore. During N----'s absence James Hensel [*Hensal*] will act as Chief of Scouts.

By order of

Brig. Gen. G. M. Dodge

J. W. Barner,

Lieut. And A.A.A.G

{Editors' Footnote: First Lieutenant John W. Barnes was the acting assistant-adjutant general for Grenville Dodge. This particular order could not be found, but Dodge did report on scouts from Pulaski in December 1863. See OR, ser. 1, vol. 32, pt. 1, p.593.}

This unverified order indicates that, at least officially, Narin was still chief of scouts until December 15, 1863. That may well have been true, since Narin's version of events was apparently told to his biographer Surby not long afterwards, certainly by 1865 when the material was first published, whereas other of the statements quoted above were not recorded until many years later, particularly those of General Dodge.

On the other hand, William Callender's recounting of another event just days before the capture of Sam Davis specifically states that James Hensal was chief of scouts at the time of the capture. Callender's story is telling because it involves a particular military action of well known date, specifically a probing attack on Knoxville which occurred on November 17, 1863, three days before the capture of Sam Davis.

Callender tells of journeying alone on horseback between Sugar Creek and Lamb's Ferry on the Tennessee River when he met a rebel sergeant. Also dressed in Confederate garb, Callender had no trouble convincing the sergeant that he was a fellow soldier.

The man said he and several of his companions were in dire need of clothing, and Callender convinced him that he could help. If the man and his four companions would meet Callender the next evening at the home of a Southerner smuggler named Carter presumably known to both men, Callender would then supply the needed clothing.

During their discussion Callender also learned that a large rebel force under the command of Longstreet had just crossed the Little Tennessee River at Louden with the intent of attacking Knoxville. Callender states in his book (pages 48-49):

> I proceeded at once to headquarters and reported what I had learned to Gen. Dodge. I may remark here in passing that the intelligence I transmitted, in reference to the meditated invasion of Knoxville by Longstreet, turned out not only to be true as an episode in the history of the war, but in point of fact it was the first intimation of the proposed attack which had been received anywhere in the Union army. The reader will comprehend at a glance how valuable this news must have been to our general officers.
>
> I then went to Hensal, who was chief of scouts [22] and reported. It was determined, on consultation, to capture the sergeant and his party. On the following day five of us, including the chief, mounted our horses and started away in the direction of Carter's residence. We rode on, until we arrived at a field, into which fresh tracks of horses, recently passing, were seen to diverge, taking: the most direct course toward the house we were seeking. We continued on the main road; and after a little time we came to a creek, half a mile from our destination. Here, in a depression of the

ground which concealed us from observation, three of us halted, while Hensal and another of our scouts whom we had given the nickname of "Bifiie," proceeded on to the proposed rendezvous.

It chanced, as our two companions who had separated from us, rode up near the house they suddenly met the rebel sergeant who, with four others, confronted them from an opposite quarter. They all drew rein in the road; and as both parties were attired in Confederate gray it was not long before the most friendly relations were instituted. After the first salutations were over Hensal turned to the sergeant, who seemed to be the leader of his party, and made to him a startling revelation:

"My friends," said our chief with great apparent earnestness, "I know where, at this very moment, and not more than half-a-mile away, three or four Yankee soldiers have halted to feed their horses. Now, as there are seven of us, we have the best chance in the world to gobble up these fellows. If you will go with me I will take you to the spot at once."

"Lead on, comrade," responded the sergeant in his innocence of the deception practiced on him; "lead on, and we will follow to the death."

Off the united party started toward the creek, Hensal being in company with the rebels, while "Biffle" rode in the lead. Meanwhile we, who had remained behind, grew weary of our protracted vigil. It was already twilight; and I was apprehensive that our well-matured plans would fail. At last, really tired and disgusted with the whole proceeding, I led my horse up the acclivity near by to make a reconnoisance.[*sic*] In the gathering gloom I saw the party moving toward us; and soon the tramp of their steeds on the highway was distinctly heard. Mounting my horse and turning for a moment to my companions, I exclaimed in suppressed tones

"My God, boys, they are coming!"

And come they did, with a rush, like that of a tornado in its wildest sweep. We formed in an instant and with a yell charged the advancing foe. An inequality in the ground, together with the dim obscurity, which began to settle on the scene, caused the steed ridden by our comrade, Norris, to fall, bringing the rider down with him, and excluding them both from any further participation in the fight. Thus reduced in strength we were outnumbered by the enemy; but Hensal, being assisted by "Bittle," Tim Foley and myself, succeeded in capturing two prisoners, one of whom was the sergeant.

The last named individual, when he saw our chief turn against him with deadly weapons, and demand his instant surrender, was livid with astonishment and terror. He was the worst sold man on the continent, and so utterly demoralized, he cried out to Hensal, in piteous accents:

"For God's sake, don't let them kill me!"

He was answered that if he told all he knew concerning the illicit and contraband traffic which was carried on by Carter, in the interest of the Confederates, his life would be spared. He made the desired promise, and when he was turned over at Pulaski he made a statement, which led promptly to the banishment of the smuggler beyond the rebel lines. We had hoped, by our ruse, to capture the sergeant's entire party, but the accident to Norris, and the closing in of night, which rendered all objects somewhat confused, gave three of the fellows a chance to get away, of which they availed themselves in a hurry.

So here is yet another bit of documentation indicating that even if Hensal was not yet officially named as chief of scouts, he certainly was acting as such, or at minimum as assistant chief of scouts at the time of the capture of Sam Davis.

Perhaps the most believable account of the Sam Davis affair because of the intricate detailing of the event, and its basis on material recorded within the next few subsequent years, is one contained in the book *Spies of the Confederacy* by John Bakeless published by Courier Dover Publications in 1998 (ISBN 0486298655, 9780486298658)[23]

Extracts from that book relating to James Hensal (on page 231):

> Having finished that secret mission, whatever it was, he [*Narin alias Chickasaw*] had returned to Dodge's headquarters and was now directing the recently enlarged Union counterintelligence group who were looking for Coleman's spies. Assisting Chickasaw in this assignment was the only slightly less formidable Sergeant James Hensal (or Hensel) of the 7th Kansas Calvary, the "Jayhawkers." Hensal's skill in military intelligence was second only to that of Chickasaw, whom he was soon to succeed as Dodge's Chief of Scouts.

Farther down the page:

> With the years, various legends have grown up around Sam Davis's capture. The facts, however, are clear enough in the sworn record of the court-martial, which has long lain forgotten among General Dodge's papers in Iowa. In these papers, the story is told by the four men who knew it first hand, testifying under oath, only a few days after the events; and it is here published for the first time. Two Union soldiers, both spies for General Dodge operating under Captain Chickasaw, and Chickasaw himself were the witnesses. Sam Davis gave his own version, which was essentially the same.
>
> Chickasaw's men, Privates Joseph E. Farrar and R. S. King, met Davis on the road about fifteen miles south of Pulaski and stopped him. All three were in Confederate uniform (except for Davis's dyed Federal overcoat, such as many Confederate soldiers wore.)

Under the guise of wanting to conscript him to serve in the Confederate army, Farrar and King took Davis to Chickasaw who was riding nearby, wearing a Confederate officer's uniform. Chickasaw questioned him enough to determine that Davis probably was an important enemy agent, and at that point, Davis thought Chickasaw actually was a Confederate officer. The account continues:

> Realizing that this unusual prisoner had better be taken back to the main body of the Union Army with as little fuss as possible, Chickasaw and at least one of his men set

out with Davis, who still may not have realized where they were taking him.

At least two of the numerous Federal reconnaissance parties that had gone out scouting that morning—in their own proper blue uniforms—were in the area toward which Chickasaw was riding, and these were soon joined by a third. Chickasaw's assistant, Sergeant James Hensal, was in the field, and so was a detachment of the 7th Kansas Calvary, the "Jayhawkers." The troopers may have been under Sergeant Hensal's command, for, though he was now on detached service, he belonged to this regiment.

At about the same time, a squad which included a soldier named John S. Randall, 66th Illinois Infantry, was coming down the road on a special mission....[*In at least one account of the affair, Randall is credited as having been one of the men who captured Sam Davis.*]

When this detachment reached a crossroads, or road junction, which Randall does not identify, the men concealed themselves in the bushes. It is clear they were somewhere near the Jayhawkers. No account of the affair explains why so many soldiers [*Randall's infantry squad and Hensal's Jayhawkers*] had to be in hiding at that particular place on that particular day.

Captor and captive rode into the Federal ambush—which Chickasaw may or may not have known was there—and both were arrested. Farrar and King seem simply to have disappeared, still in rebel uniform. Hensal says he saw only two men riding down the road. Chickasaw says he had three men with him—that is, Farrar, King, and Davis—but he does not say he had them with him all the time. He does not say how he identified himself. Hensal, of course, knew him well.

At 10:20 a.m. Nov. 27, 1863, Coleman Scout Sam Davis was dropped from the gallows and hanged. Union soldier John Randal[l], who had helped capture Davis, watched with tears streaming down his face as the young Tennessean was executed. He later stated that he had never witnessed such a pathetic and heroic scene and noted other Federal soldiers in tears.[24]

Putting all these stories together, it seems likely that we now have a most probable accounting of the likely relationship between James A. Hensal and Levi H. Narin (Chickasaw) at the time of the Sam Davis affair, and the role of each of them and others credited with Davis's capture. General Grenville Dodge credited Hensal with the capture, and Narin credited himself. Both appear to be correct to the extent that perhaps Davis was "captured" twice. The initial capture was by Privates Joseph E. Farrar and R. S. King acting under the overall direction of Chief of Scouts Levi Narin and perhaps reporting to him through his Assistant Chief of Scouts James Hensal. Then shortly thereafter Hensal "captured" Sam Davis a second time, along with his boss Narin. One man said to be involved in the capture, John Randall, was involved only peripherally, in his role as part of the ambush along the road.

As to exactly what happened, it mostly comes down to the word of General Dodge versus that of Narin. I have not found any evidence of Hensal having said anything about the matter. Obviously, neither Narin nor Hensal had any direct connection with Davis' capture, other than through chain of command. The actual capture evidently was by soldiers R. S. King and Joseph E. Farrar.

The overall result is that we have contradictory information on the actual date of Hensal becoming chief of scouts, but the bulk of the evidence suggests that King and Farrar were under his direct command when they captured Sam Davis on November 20, 1863. Regardless of the exact details, this story helps clarify that James Hensal was a major player in the Civil War, and it adds to the significance of the previously unknown painting of him by Hood.

IMPACT OF THIS SEARCH ON THE APPRAISAL OF THE PAINTING

⌒ᴍ⌒

Jane C. H. Jacob completed her initial "Fair Market Value Appraisal for Planning Purposes" of the painting in October 2005 on the basis of photographs and other documentation available at the time. That appraisal resulted in assigning to the painting a slightly lower value than assigned by her in the final appraisal completed in June 2010, one titled "Fair Market Value Appraisal for Non-cash Charitable Contribution Purposes." By then she had been able to view the painting directly and have an art expert verify that the painting had been properly restored and that it and its frame were in good condition. Also at that time she had available most, but not quite all, of the information uncovered by this investigation. The most significant lack was verification of the interesting story regarding Hensal's killing his superior officer Capt. Fred Swoyer, for which a court-martial sentenced him to death, the subsequent signing of the death warrant by Abraham Lincoln, and how all this caused Hensal to become a scout for General Grenville Dodge.

According to the initial "Fair Market Appraisal" prepared by Jane C. H. Jacob in 2005, a number of criteria go into establishing the value of a painting such as this:

1—The name, reputation and market status of the artist, 2—The desirability of the style in today's market, 3—Medium and technique. 4—Subject matter, 5—Date of execution or time period, 6—Dimensions, 7—Signature and where located, 8—Current fashion of collectors, 9—Historical significance, 10—Provenance, 11—Rarity, 12—Quality, 13—Bibliography references and exhibition history, and 14—Condition problems, previous restorations.

In her appraisal reports Jane C. H. Jacob made specific note of several issues affecting valuation of the painting. Among them was the fact that the artist, John H. G. Hood, was a self-taught artist with sufficient talent to make his living as a painter and artist but had only local reputation as an artist and painter, and that the painting of Hensal is his only known major work still in existence. According to Ms. Jacob, this painting is in the style of "folk painting," also called "naïve" or "primitive" and "demonstrates a degree of sophistication in the artist's work in pleasing colors and a sense of vitality that is very attractive." Also, this is a rare painting in various respects. The fact that it is painted on an old-fashioned window blind makes it unique in the known examples of Civil War paintings. It is significant that the painting depicts an actual event in the conflict, and is of a known subject, a colorful, daring and fearless individual who was an important figure in the war. The painting is the only one known that depicts a Northern soldier in a Confederate uniform. Unusual also is the fact that we have available images of the artist's pencil sketchbook containing a sketch which obviously is one on which the painting is based.

Adding to the value is the well known provenance of the painting. Originally it was owned by its subject James A. Hensal who presumably received it from the artist as a gift or for services rendered, perhaps for providing post-war housing and sustenance during a period when artist Hood was financially distressed. James Hensal passed the picture to his son Telford, who passed it on to his son Irwin, and after his death, Irwin's wife Louphena gave it to me, her nephew. As noted before, I first became acquainted with the painting in the early 1940s. The painting has been well cared for over the years, having for most or all of its life been protected from direct sunlight by being hung in dark rooms or hallways. When I acquired the painting in the 1990s it had two small age-related tears in the window blind and some overall craquelure. In 2001, I had restorer Barbara Engstrom of Northshore Art Conservation, Port Townsend, Washington, put a canvas backing on the widow blind. In fall 2007, I delivered the painting to Jane Jacob, at which time it was examined by an art expert who decreed that the restoration was proper, and that the painting and frame were in good condition. It remained in her possession until June 2010. At the time we gifted the painting to the Guthrie County Historical Museum at Panora, Iowa. Thus, after more than a century, the painting returned to its birthplace, and its first viewing by the public.

Jane Jacob's fair market appraisal report completed on June 25, 2010, stated that she looked at recently sold paintings of similar nature to establish a base price that she would then adjust up or down by considering various relevant issues. Out of sixteen Civil War paintings sold since 2000 she picked one she considered as most relevant, a painting by Richard Gaul of a battle scene painted in 1865 that had sold for approximately $150,000. This painting was 1.5 times larger than Hood's painting of Hensal, so she set the base price for Hood's painting at $100,000, the figure to be adjusted up or down according to various factors.

Owners of the painting after James Hensal, left to right, Janie Hensal (wife of Telford) 2nd owner Telford Hensal, his daughter Dorothy, 4th owner Louphena (Davis) Hensal, Harold Hensal (son of Telford), and 3rd owner Irwin Hensal. Photographed August 1928 at time of marriage of Irwin and Louphena.

It was mostly a roller coaster ride from there, yet one ending on a positive note:

The fact that Hood was an unknown artist knocked $40,000 off the value of the painting.

That the medium he chose was unusual—an old-fashioned window blind well preserved—upped the value by $30,000.

The general aesthetic nature of the painting lowered the value by $30,000.

The date of execution in the 19th century upped the value by $30,000.

The quality of execution and composition of the painting lowered the value by $30,000.

The well known provenance of the painting upped the value by $20,000.

The rarity of the painting added another $20,000.

The fact that a reproduction of the painting was published in a reputable book added $20,000.

And finally, the significance of the subject, that he was a nationally known historical figure, upped the value by $75,000.

The end result of these pluses and minuses was the final assignment of $127,500 for what we initially thought was a worthless painting. So from a monetary point of view, this investigation into the background of the artist and his subject definitely was worthwhile, and it certainly was fun to see new information develop and often lead to yet other previously unknown.

Interestingly enough, some of the information presented here came to light after Jane Jacob's final appraisal of the painting. That includes verification that James Hensal actually did shoot and kill his superior officer Fred Swoyer, plus a determination of the date and most probable circumstances of the event.

As time goes by, perhaps enough more may be learned about Hood and Hensal to remove some of the perhaps inconsequential uncertainties that still remain. One regards the true date of the painting. Did John Hood come to live on Hensal's farm and execute the painting of him shortly after the Civil War, as is suggested by family lore, or did he paint Hensal much later, sometime after 1890?

Another uncertainty is about the relationship between James Hensal and Levi Narin at the time of the capture and execution of Sam Davis. Was Hensal still reporting to Narin at this time, or had he already succeeded him as General Dodge's chief of scouts?

Other perhaps unimportant issues nag the mind as well. In particular are instances where various accounts of one event appear to bring in details of what probably was some other event or suggest uncertainty about the relationship of one event to another.

A good example is the ride into enemy forces Hensal describes in his long letter written in 1907 to General Dodge. According to this letter, the ride took place one night in October 1862 at the request of Capt. Fred Swoyer. At that time Hensal had yet to be formally assigned to scouting duties and was under arrest, presumably by order of Capt. Swoyer. Hensal's letter states that he went out once but came back and demanded a fresh horse on which to ride out again. It is a bit unnerving that George Kenan's account of a later ride contains a few of the same details. In that account, Hensal also was under arrest, but this time after being sentenced to death for killing Capt. Swoyer on January 3, 1963. Again, Hensal asked for a horse, again was carrying a dispatch, and the ride also was at night. Was all this coincidence, or perhaps had Kenan heard the story of the earlier ride and mixed some of its details into his telling of the ride ordered by General Dodge and which presumably started Hensal's career as a scout? My guess is that this is what happened, but in either case the parallels in the two accounts are a bit disconcerting. It is a reminder that we cannot place complete trust in our knowledge of the details of events described long afterwards. Which brings me back to the point made earlier regarding the "quantum mechanics" nature of the history of minor events and the doings of individuals—an element of uncertainty seems always to persist.

Nevertheless, investigations into the actions of persons who lived long ago can be rather sporting, and for those who contemplate them I give a few procedural hints in the Appendix.

Appendix—Procedural Hints

⌣⁀⌣

The Internet is a powerful tool for obtaining information about almost everything. It's basically free, and it is getting better by the day as more books and other documents are made available through digitization. It is now possible to search inside many publications for information about individuals and events. Changes are happening so rapidly that repeating an earlier search on a word or phrase a few weeks later may yield new results.

It is wise to try to verify dates, events, or other information by exploring multiple Internet or other sources because spelling and dating errors do occur in the sources.

Google and perhaps other search engines are both forgiving and helpful as they give alternate spellings to words you search on if the engine thinks you might have erred. Sometimes that helps you obtain new information.

Do not hesitate to search on names that persons or documents refer to but which initially appear to be of minor relevance. That can uncover unsuspected treasures of relevant information.

Be suspicious of oral statements made well after the fact. They are perhaps true, but if they have gone through several retellings, the end results probably are not quite correct, even though they may tell the essence of the story. That's why historians prefer primary rather than secondary accounts.

The same is true of written material. Most trustworthy are written descriptions of events made near the time of the events by persons involved. But be aware that their bias may color the descriptions.

About the author: Neil Davis is an emeritus professor of geophysics at the University of Alaska Fairbanks where his scientific career has dealt primarily with studies of the aurora, and also seismology. He is the author of several fiction and nonfiction books and for some years wrote a weekly science newspaper column. Currently he writes a monthly column on health care finances and related topics. Davis and his wife Rosemarie live near the University of Alaska Fairbanks campus in an owner-built home they started constructing in 1956 and which is almost finished.

References and Notes

1. Lotter, David, Grenville Dodge (1831-1916), Signal Corps Association, 1860-65 http://www.civilwarsignals.org/pages/spy/pages/dodge.html. (Accessed 11/11/2010)

2. Copied by Elaine Lundberg of Panora, Iowa, from the Guthrie County Iowa, Records: Misc. Land Deed Book "A" page 120 during July 2010, it having been filed there by James Hensal on February 6, 1867.

3. http://skyways.lib.ks.us/genweb/archives/statewide/military/civilwar/adjutant/7/b.html (Accessed 09/10/2010)

4. http://www.ku.edu/about/traditions/jayhawk.shtml (Accessed 09/10/2010)

5. Kerrihard, Bowen, America's Civil War: Missouri and Kansas, *America's Civil War*, March 1999, See at: http://www.historynet.com/americas-civil-war-missouri-and-kansas.htm (Accessed 09/10/2010)

6. Goodrich, Thomas, Black Flag: Guerilla Warfare on the Western Border, 1861-1865, University of Indiana Press: Bloomington, 1995, p 16. Quoted at http://www.moksbwn.net/images/JayhawkBrochure.pdf. (Accessed 09/10/2010)

7. Remsburg, George J., an article published in the *Leavenworth Times* in 1942, See at: http://skyways.lib.ks.us/genweb/leavenwo/library/7CAVARY.htm (Accessed 09/10/2010)

8. Kansas Historical Society, See: http://www.kshs.org/p/seventh-regiment-jennison-s-jayhawkers-kansas-volunteer-cavalry/11173. (Accessed 11/08/2010)

9. Dr. William Feis sent me a copy of this letter in July 2005. The original is in Box 14?? of the Grenville M. Dodge Papers archived in Des Moines, Iowa.

10. Illinois Immigrant Heroes of the Civil War: http://www.lib.niu.edu/1994//ihy940232.html. (Accessed 09/10/2010)

11. http://battleofraymond.org/command4.htm. (Accessed 11/09/2010)

12. http://en.wikipedia.org/wiki/Thomas_William_Sweeny (Accessed 09/10/2010)

13. http://www.civilwarhome.com/Pay.htm (Accessed 09/10/2010)

14. http://files.usgwarchives.org/ia/polk/history/1898/annalsof/polkcoun33nms.txt (Accessed 10/02/2010)

15. Ref: http://www.panora.org/museum/index_files/local_history.htm (Accessed 11/05/2010)

16. In *Struggle for a vast future, the American Civil War*, edited by Aaron Sheehan-Dean, (Oxford: United Kingdom, Osprey Publishing Ltd. 2006 (ISBN 1-84603-011-0), pages 152-53 and 160)

17. http://www.artcirclelibrary.info/Reference/civilwar/1863-01.pdf , pages 12-14 (Accessed 10/02/2010)

18. Ibid, pages 14-15.

19. Ibid, page 15.

20. Fox, S. M. (Simeon M.), Story of the Seventh Kansas, Kansas State Historical Society, The Kansas Historical Quarterly, Volume 23, See: http://books.google.com/books?id=QibTKncC2VUC&dq=%22Fred+S woyer%22&source=gbs_navlinks_s . (Accessed 11/08/2010)

21. www.civilwarhome.com/roddey4alacav.htm (Accessed 10/02/2010)

22. Longstreet crossed the river on November 14, 1863, so this event must have occurred on that day or within a day or two later. After the crossing on November 14, 1863, Longstreet made a probing attack on Knoxville on November 17, with the main battle commencing on November 29. See: http://tennesseeencyclopedia.net/imagegallery.php?EntryID=K018. (Accessed 09/10/2010) Thus, according to Callender, James Hensal was chief of scouts prior to November 17, 1863. The capture of Sam Davis was two or three days later.

23. However a hint of a warning about cited sources is given in a review of the book:, "No mean historian, Bakeless nonetheless likes a good story well enough to rely on somewhat dubious documentation (though these sources are often indicated right in the text). But on the whole, the history's sound and adventures abound - in spy ring exploits with period-piece appeal." (Kirkus Reviews)

24. The story of Sam Davis, Tennessee History Classroom, http://www.vic.com/tnchron/class/SamDavis.htm (Accessed 09/10/2010)

INDEX